GREY
FUNNEL LINES
TRADITIONAL SONG & VERSE OF
THE ROYAL NAVY 1900-1970

The Grey Funnel Line

Don't mind the rain or the rolling sea,
The weary night never worries me,
But the hardest time in a sailor's day
Is to watch the sun as it dies away.

> It's one more day
> On the Grey Funnel Line.

The finest ship that sailed the sea
Is still a prison to the likes of me,
But give me wings like Noah's dove
I'd fly up harbour to the girl I love.

> It's one more day
> On the Grey Funnel Line.

There was a time my heart was free,
Like a floating spar on the open sea,
But now the spar is washed ashore,
It come's to rest at my real love's door.

> It's one more day
> On the Grey Funnel Line.

Every time I gaze behind the screws
Makes me long for old Peter's shoes,
I'd walk right down that silver lane
And take my love in my arms again.

> It's one more day
> On the Grey Funnel Line.

Oh Lord, if dreams were only real
I'd have my hands on that wooden wheel
And with all my heart I'd turn her round
And tell the boys that we're homeward bound.

> It's one more day
> On the Grey Funnel Line.

I'll pass the time like some machine
Until the blue water turns to green,
Then I'll dance on down that walk-ashore,
And sail the Grey Funnel Line no more.

> And sail the Grey
> Funnel Line no more.

Cyril Tawney (1959)
Copyright Gwyneth Music Ltd

GREY
FUNNEL LINES
TRADITIONAL SONG & VERSE OF
THE ROYAL NAVY 1900-1970

Routledge & Kegan Paul

London

First published in 1987 by
Routledge & Kegan Paul Ltd
11 New Fetter Lane, London EC4P 4EE

Set in 11½/12½pt Garamond
by Columns of Reading
and printed in Great Britain
by T.J. Press (Padstow) Ltd
Padstow, Cornwall

British Library Cataloguing in Publication Data

Grey funnel lines: traditional song and
verse of the Royal Navy, 1900-1970
  1. Sea songs, English
  I. Tawney, Cyril
  784.6'86238   PR1195.S417

ISBN 0-7102-1270-4

This book is dedicated to the memory of

ANDREW LEES
(1943–1970)

Sailor,
Folk Singer,
Good Companion

CONTENTS

CONTENTS

PREFACE

Preparing this collection for publication has involved decid-
ing on a number of policies which I believe need explaining if not
defending. First there was the difficulty of coming to terms with the
fact that, unlike the majority of previous folk song collectors, I was
working to a certain extent with texts which I had never heard
performed, sent to me by people I had never met. Long experience
has led me to a conclusion which will surprise many, namely that the
ability of singers to transcribe a song on to paper word-for-word
exactly as they sing it is far less common than might be supposed. In
the past, if doubts have arisen as regards scansion or some other
aspect of the text, I have, where the opportunity has presented itself,
asked the transcriber to sing the song, only to find in many cases that
in their transcriptions they have omitted the occasional minor word
or made other slight alterations which, though retaining the full
sense of the verse, have done considerable injury to its metre. I recall
one instance where this happened with a song actually written by the
singer himself. (It is a point also to be borne in mind by students of
medieval lyrics written down by scribes whose chief concern may
have been preservation rather than performance.) Another consider-
ation is that many people who supply the words of songs in
manuscript form are not themselves singers at all. They may never
have actually performed the songs, even to their intimates. Their role
has been simply that of a passive listener who liked a particular song
and heard it often enough, or had a good enough memory, to retain
the bulk of the words in their head. Under the normal 'folk process',
had they then performed the song they would have patched up any
textual discrepancies by improvisation. As it is, they have probably

in many cases passed on the words that they remember, in manuscript form and with the discrepancies retained. As a consequence I have in some places felt justified in employing what scholars have called an 'educated imagination' in restoring a line to what I believe was the most likely form in which it was sung. I hope this will not be construed as tampering with tradition. Rather, it is a case of trying to estimate the amount of 'tampering' that has already taken place and attempting, with insight, to undo it.

In one respect a contributor's alterations have been quite deliberate. I refer to the delicate matter of the expletives and gross terminology in common usage among seafarers and others. However much they may make use of an obscene vocabulary themselves there are many men, especially those of the old school, who cannot bring themselves to transfer such words to paper for perusal by a complete stranger. They either leave blanks or substitute innocuous alternatives such as 'blooming', 'blinking' or 'flipping'. While respecting their reserve, I feel that to reproduce such modifications would be to dissipate the essential vigour of the sailor's idiom and falsify the evidence regarding his typical modes of expression. On the other hand, Jack himself has a small and potently variable range of utterances from which he chooses freely, and what has come to be regarded as the ultimate expletive is not always used. I have chosen, therefore, to select where feasible the word 'bleeding', a term which is at once relatively inoffensive to the majority yet retains much of the bite associated with stronger terms. It is a middle course which I hope offends the fewest sensitivities. None the less I have felt compelled to retain any word whose omission would affect either rhyme or alliteration, or would in any other way be detrimental to the lyric.

Times change. We live now in a world where certain attitudes, if not substantially different from those prevalent in the days when most of these songs were composed, are at least not flaunted so offensively nor tolerated so meekly. For instance, some of the old-time sailor's songs about women would now drop quite easily into the 'sexist' bracket. Yet those who man (?) the feminist barricades should not be taken in too readily by these outward displays of male chauvinism. In *Three Corvettes* (Cassell, 1945) Nicholas Monsarrat gives us a much truer picture of how things really are:

When men are cooped up together at close quarters, the tone of conversation does not exactly reflect a humble worship at the shrine of womanhood: there is a lot of loose talk (some of it exceptionally loose) about 'torpedoing' and other inelegant exploits, and a chance listener might reasonably suppose that he had to deal with a nest of old-fashioned rogues of the 'Yield-or-else' type. And when several ratings are together ashore they are inclined to behave badly, chi-iking girls and generally embarrassing them. But separate one of them, and put him on his own with exactly the same girl, and he usually becomes a model of deference and attention. It is only when he is with a crowd that he lacks the courage or the initiative to treat women as normal human beings.

Similarly, ethnic susceptibilities have now proscribed words such as 'wog' and 'nigger', but in former years terms like this would fall from a matelot's lips without a second thought, and it is no surprise to find them occurring, albeit very rarely, in the songs he sang in those days. No malice was intended. Every ethnic group was accorded its nickname, and it is unfortunate that connotations linked with an epithet in the Southern States of America should have reverberated to such regrettable effect in more racially tolerant areas. Once again, with all due apologies to those who find such a measure offensive, I have preferred in the interests of documentary accuracy to let the record stand. (As it happens, in this collection only two songs are involved, a fact which I hope speaks for itself.)

It may puzzle some readers to find the background material to the songs presented virtually throughout in the past tense. I have adopted this policy simply because my knowledge of today's Royal Navy is so scant that I might well be misleading people if I persisted in saying 'this happens' or 'that happens'. Much of what I refer to may still apply, of course, but as the major part of the collection comes from what must now be considered a bygone age I feel on much safer ground in treating it from a retrospective viewpoint.

As far as possible I have given the name of the tune to which the words were sung. Where no tune is indicated it is because: (a) the tune has not been communicated to me and I have been unable to discover it; (b) the words in question were not sung but recited or chanted; or (c) the song (and there are very few) has a tune of its own. I have included most of these as an Appendix. It is hoped that one or more long-playing records and/or cassettes containing a selection of the songs will be produced to coincide with this publication, so that these tunes will be more available to the non-musical.

Should a given song title be unfamiliar to the reader, the song publisher's name and address can usually be obtained from: Copyright Department, The Performing Right Society Ltd, 29/33 Berners Street, LONDON W1P 4AA; tel. 01-580-5544. It should then be possible to obtain a copy of the sheet-music for the tune in question either through a music shop or direct from the song publisher concerned. However, it should not then be assumed that the words given will fit the tune like a glove. There is often a considerable amount of adaptation to be done, and in many cases it would perhaps be more accurate to regard the actual tune used as being merely 'based on' the one named.

'Villikins and his Dinah' is one of the best known English popular tunes, and is used for numerous songs, for instance 'The Threshing Machine'.

ACKNOWLEDGMENTS

In the following pages the reader will find I have referred to myself as 'the author'. This has been done only for economy of expression, the more accurate description of 'collector, collator, compiler and editor' being as unwieldy as the poor old 'K'-class submarine which features in song No. 81.

It will soon become obvious who the true 'authors' are, and my primary gratitude must be to them. They are of two kinds. There are the more specific ex-Navy men and women who took the trouble to ransack their ditty-box (how apt a name) of Service memories and communicate what they found there. Many of their names I know and have duly recorded. But there have been scores of others whose song-offering was an anonymous act; nothing more than a casual, spontaneous gesture of social generosity amid, maybe, the stuffy smoke-haze of some squalid, long-forgotten sailor-town tavern, or the spartan bleakness of a take-it-or-leave-it NAAFI bar anywhere between Scapa Flow and Malta; or even, later on, the grey-templed, blue-blazered bonhomie of an RNA gathering. As often as not their nameless benevolence might have been totally swilled from my mind by the excesses of the occasion but for the discovery, on going through my pockets the morning after, of a spidery stanza or two scrawled across a fag-packet, beer-mat, diary memo-page or paper napkin. These vague, faceless spectres from my ramblesome past have as much right as anyone else to be ranked among the salvors of the Navy's songs. And, for all I know, those few lines from a lurching hand may have been the only lasting testimony some of them would leave to the world.

Behind these actual informants, sunk in even deeper anonymity, stands that nebulous throng of naval personnel who, decades before the collector and preserver came on the scene, kept these songs alive with nothing but their voices, memory and enthusiasm. Among them, inevitably, would have been the 'prime movers', men like John Bush (song No. 27) and Captain Cunningham and his colleagues (No. 69), who constructed, out of their own predicament and imagination, the prototypes for succeeding songsters to adopt and adapt. There must even now be many people, unknown to me but still living, who will read these pages and recognise either their own handiwork or something remarkably similar. I hope they will understand that no plagiarism was intended, and that the songs, having earned the accolade of being wholly accepted into the Royal Navy's oral tradition and being untraceable, except in the cases cited, to any known author, have been included here in good faith.

My thanks are due to several organs of the press for lending impetus to the collecting process, albeit with varying success: to Edwin Burrows and the *Hampshire Telegraph* who launched my first appeal all those years ago, then to *Navy News* not only for publishing my second request for songs but for later responding in such lively fashion to Commander Peter Williams's similar enquiry. In passing on to me the results of that campaign Commander Williams has left me forever in his debt.

Both the *Western Morning News* and *Western Evening Herald* of Plymouth helped to arouse public awareness of Navy songs from time to time, either through their columns or by publishing my writings on the subject, as did the now defunct magazine *Folk Review* edited by Fred Woods.

Mention of *Folk Review* reminds me that in at least one respect this book is unique. It is the first serious collection of traditional songs part of which, however small, has been gathered as a direct result of the Second Folk Revival and its associated folk club movement. Several of the songs, and extra verses to others, were actually acquired from members of folk club audiences, during or following my appearances as guest singer. The same movement has also been instrumental in affording me, through my occupation as a full-time professional, the necessary mobility to travel the length and breadth of the land year after year with my song enquiries (it should not be imagined that every song was picked up within earshot of the seashore). I therefore feel a special 'thank you' is due to all those who laboured to keep open those weekly song-markets in so many towns and cities throughout the UK, with no idea, nor in most cases any hope, of personal profit. I hope they will derive some satisfaction from the knowledge that this volume is, to a limited extent, one of the more positive and durable by-products of their efforts.

Whenever I was in doubt about meanings of terms, or any other information relating to naval matters which lay outside my own experience, I knew I could rely on the staff of the National Maritime Museum at Greenwich or the Fleet Air Arm Museum at Yeovilton to do their utmost to come up with the answer. Certain individuals, too, in particular Shep Woolley, Tony Haynes, Nigel Matimong, Lt.Cdr. Norman Dubery, RNVSR and Lt-Col. Sir Vivian Dunn, KCVO, OBE, FRAM, RM, gave me the benefit of their specialised knowledge in areas that would otherwise have left me baffled.

Preparation of the typescript, involving wave upon wave of alterations, deletions and additions stretching over a far longer period than first anticipated, has induced a quite astonishing display of sustained patience and good humour on the part of Barbara Binless and her husband Grahame. Similar forbearance was frequently required of my wife Rosemary, who also brought her own dedication to such jobs as listing the Index and helping, from a most valuable lay viewpoint, in the far less straightforward task of marshalling the terms featured in the Glossary. And how much longer the book would have taken to complete had she been unable or unwilling to don the mantle of principal breadwinner while I took the necessary sabbatical I cannot begin to estimate.

I am grateful to John Large for copying out the music for publication and bringing professional respectability to my own novice transcriptions.

The Sociology Department of Lancaster University, and Suzette Heald in particular, deserve my thanks for long ago nursing me through a first year dissertation from which the book's Introduction and 'Sternpiece' are derived.

Even earlier the poet Charles Causley played an important part, too, in being the first to convince me, over a couple of beers in a Cornish pub in the late 1960s, of the value of what I was collecting and the need for its publication.

For permission to include extracts and songs from their publications my gratitude is extended to the following: *The News*, Portsmouth, for 'Coal Ship Song II', 'Roll on the Aeroplane Navy' and the quote on pp. 19-20, all from a *Hampshire Telegraph* article;

Campbell Thomson & McLaughlin Ltd for *Three Corvettes* by Nicholas Monsarrat; Century Hutchinson Ltd for 'P.Q.17' by Godfrey Winn; EFDS publications and Clare Clayton for 'Sailors' Wives'; A. P. Watt Ltd for *Endless Story* by Capt. Taprell Dorling RN; Inglis Gundry for 'Russian Convoy Escort's Song'; Harry Lockey ('Folk Roundabout') for 'Hospital Ship Song'; Grafton Books for 'Twelve Little "S"-Boats' from *One of our Submarines* by Edward Young; William Kimber & Co. Ltd for *British Submarines at War 1939-45* by Alastair Mars; Manchester University Press for *The Lower Deck of the Royal Navy 1900-1939* by Anthony Carew.

Photographs are reproduced by permission of the Imperial War Museum.

Roy Palmer was good enough to divert some of his valuable time, during the preparation of his own *Oxford Book of Sea Songs*, in order to furnish me with recordings of some ex-RN singers in his area, as well as hunting up other queries I had.

One more 'Acknowledgment' remains. My ultimate thanks, at least as far as this book is concerned, must be offered up to a Providence which not only blessed my brother and me with a home-town environment saturated with all things Navy, the good and the bad, but also favoured us with parents who refused to subscribe to the maxim 'not in front of the children'. These two factors ensured that when it came to soaking up the lore and jargon of the messdeck we had several lengths' start on youngsters whose introduction to such mysteries was deferred until after they had passed through the Recruiting Office. All books are preceded by a period of gestation, some much longer than others. At what point the process began in my case is impossible to determine, but inasmuch as such an upbringing gave me an early taste for what has turned out to be the foundation and substance of this anthology, a non-naval childhood might have delayed its fruition by a dozen years or more, by which time who knows how many of these songs would have slipped through our fingers for good?

Cyril Tawney

Whenever I see 'prim goodness' frown at the rough, careless sailor's oath that will mingle now and then with his 'ye-ho!' I think to myself 'Take out your heart, "prim goodness", and lay it by the side of Jack's and offer me the choice of the two, and maybe it won't be yours I'll take, for all that you are faultless to the world's eye.'

FRANK MARRYAT, Mountains and Molehills, London, 1855

Ne al soh ne al les that leod-scopes singeth.
('What the people's poets sing is neither all truth nor all lies.')

Layamon's Brut, circa 1200

INTRODUCTION

'Where, then, is the theme for song?' –
The singing sailor in the twentieth century

The day of Real Sailor Songs is long since past and gone. They died
out with the old French war, and its consequent peace. In the old war
they were at their best, and they died in their prime. They were
odorous of the sea, because they were of it, and they were part and
parcel of the life thereon. They are dead, and the songs sung by sailors
nowadays come direct from Music Halls.

> JOHN ASHTON, preface to *Real Sailor Songs*, London 1891

It is not to be expected that people who deal solely with ship's engines
and boilers, or with the many electrical and mechanical appliances
now installed afloat, would appreciate the charm of a wind that filled
the white and rustling sail and bent the gallant mast. Sweet William
now would be less likely to be found high upon the yard than deep
down in the stokehold or submerged torpedo-flat. For these important
sections of modern crews there are no traditional songs and they have
to take over their minstrelsy ready-made from the music halls.

> SIR CYPRIAN BRIDGE, Introduction to Christopher Stone's
> *Sea Songs and Ballads*, Oxford, 1906

The Romance of the sea is gone, and with it are gone Sea Songs.
Piracy and privateering are impossible: so are 'carrying on', reefing
topsails, and all the many things which gave romance to the sailor's
life. Where, then, is the theme for song? . . . Since 1872 I have not
heard a shanty or song worth the name. Steam spoilt them. A younger

1

generation of seamen took the place of the old sea-dog. The real thing has gone forever.

CAPTAIN W. B. WHALL, *Sea Songs and Shanties*, Glasgow, 1920

Today's sailor on leave, in his civvy clothes, could be mistaken for a salesman or an off-duty policeman. He doesn't know any yarns, really, and he couldn't tell a shanty from a shoehorn.

WILLIAM COLE, Introduction to *The Sea, Ships and Sailors*,
Rupert Hart-Davis, 1968

As a chain of situation reports on the state of Royal Naval song-making the above make dismal reading, but they represent a belief widely held throughout the three-quarters of a century which they cover. Moreover, while it would be easy for me, with the advantage of hindsight, to scoff at such pessimism, it was a view I felt inclined to agree with when in 1958 I first applied myself seriously to the question 'Where, if they exist at all, are the Royal Navy folk songs of the ironclad era?' Fortunately I recalled a remark made by the American guitarist Les Paul concerning the wisest piece of advice given him as a young man: 'Never say you can't until you've proved you can't.' I imagined that Mr Paul's mentor, faced with my problem, would have adapted his precept to: 'Never say there aren't any songs until you've proved there aren't,' so I decided to do what the writers quoted above appear not to have done. I started to ask. And went on asking.

I probably would never have bothered had I not already acquired a few songs and snatches at first hand, firstly from my father in my youth, and later, during my own naval service, from other RN personnel. It occurred to me that if I had gleaned that many without even trying then a more single-minded approach might yield a few more.

From the beginning I set myself the following criteria:

1 The songs had to have originated in the twentieth century, or at least since the days of Royal Navy sailing ships were over. Some songs of the sail era were carried over into steam, naturally, and I was glad to recover them when I could (see Appendix A), but I would not consider them to be folk songs from the modern Royal Navy.

2 To counter any suggestion that the modern sailor's repertoire was a second-hand one, borrowed from other sources and only

slightly adapted for his own use, no songs known to be part of a shared repertoire (and these are plentiful, see Appendix B) sung with minimal alterations by other groups or fraternities such as the Army, RAF, students, rugby players and so on, would be considered to be Royal Navy songs. The mere conversion of another two-syllable word such as 'soldier', 'pongo', 'airman' or 'student' into 'sailor' or 'matelot' would be insufficient for an item to merit the description 'Royal Navy'. The distinction is a fine one and not easy to establish. Once any song has been re-worked sufficiently it takes on a separate existence of its own and, in that form, can be said to have been freshly created, but often a Judgment of Solomon is called for. The determining factor may perhaps be best illustrated by an examination of two border-line cases. 'The Tenth MTB Flotilla Song' (No. 103) is clearly related to 'We're Looking for the Kaiser' (No. 63), and both are well laced with Navy references. But whereas the former is merely a counterpart of the military 'We are Fred Karno's Army', with only minor word substitutions, the latter does not merge in any way with the Army song until halfway through. Its first half is quite distinctive. (There may be an Army equivalent of these first four lines but I am not aware that one exists.) 'We're Looking for the Kaiser', therefore, just scrapes into the Royal Navy category while 'The Tenth MTB Flotilla Song' has to be considered part of a shared repertoire.

Admittedly in adopting this principle an element of unfairness is involved. Even songs in a shared repertoire have to start somewhere, and among those excluded from the collection proper there must be some, like 'Sod 'Em All' (No. 107), that originated among naval personnel and were later taken over and adapted by other sections of society. Proving which ones these are, however, is another matter entirely, and at least such a system of selection allows the claim to be put forward that those songs remaining are undeniably out-and-out Navy products.

3 I was concerned in the main with a creative singing tradition. Therefore, to warrant its inclusion, there must be some evidence, however slender, that a song had been, to some degree at least, circulated orally. This is more difficult to establish when only one version of a song has been collected than when several variants are available. In some cases I have had to rely solely on the contributor's own testimony or verbal assurances from others that a song was fairly regularly sung and passed around by word of mouth. Without such a specification, however, it would have been impossible to ignore the

countless ditties composed, say, for a particular concert or revue, thereafter to be discarded like squeezed lemons, or the many admirable contributions printed in ship and shore establishment magazines which, as far as can be ascertained, were never adopted for singing purposes by Navy personnel and existed solely in print ('Corrosions has Set In', No. 19, appears to have been one exception, though more evidence to this effect would be welcome). The citing of a body of literature, however substantial and no matter how popular, is no evidence of a creative singing tradition.

Like many song collectors before and since I found the press willing to help. In December 1960, through the medium of Edwin Burrow's 'Stanchion' column in the *Hampshire Telegraph*, the first appeal for RN songs was made. The response was disappointing, and very little worthwhile was gathered. In September 1966, in the correspondence column of *Navy News*, I made a second appeal. There was a slight improvement on 1960, but the reaction was still not encouraging. An article of mine on RN songs published in the *Western Morning News* on 12 March 1970 brought forth only one fresh song. I was finding that my own first-hand collecting was producing far better results than appeals via the press.

Then, in May 1970, the *Navy News*, for what reason I have not been able to discover, suddenly decided to sit up and take more notice, not as a result of any approach of mine, but because of a letter on the subject from Commander Peter Williams. For the next seven issues, from May to November, the paper ran a song-collecting campaign covering up to half a page each issue. Although the amount of genuine RN material gathered disappointed Commander Williams and did not in his opinion warrant the publication of a book, compared with the reactions to my own previous efforts in the press the response was quite impressive. In the course of time Commander Williams generously passed over to me the songs he had received, and while it was true that on their own they did not form a very significant corpus of material, as an augmentation of my own collection they proved very useful.

The contributors have nearly all been ex-RN, occasionally former members of the WRNS, and their periods of service cover the major part of the first seven decades of the twentieth century. What seems to have disappeared, assuming he ever existed even in the days of sail, is the sailor with a large repertoire of authentic RN folk songs. Most informants contributed between one and six acceptable items. Thus,

4

if evidence is based on one or two encounters with individual naval people the wrong conclusions are likely to be drawn, and this indication of a fragmented repertoire may readily account for the misconceptions concerning the modern sailor and his songs evidenced in the quotations at the head of this Introduction.

One frequently hears of a singer with a large repertoire, someone who could 'sing matelot's songs all night without repeating himself'. More often than not the informant will assure you he was 'on my last ship' (everything worthwhile happened on a sailor's previous ship). But one never actually meets such a man, and all efforts to trace him usually end in a blank or disappointment at finding the informant had greatly overstated things. Either time and distance have lent enchantment to the song-tally or its contents are not as strictly 'Navy' as the stated criteria require.

Singing in the Royal Navy is mostly, though not wholly, an off-duty pastime. The majority of the songs collected date from pre-1945, an era of large ships and massive fleets, and in this period it was no uncommon sight to find a fleet canteen in an otherwise quiet spot, such as Invergordon or Scapa Flow, or a sailor's club in a major naval port, thronging with perhaps 500–2000 sailors at a time. When contributors gave information as to where and when the songs would be sung it was to these places that they chiefly referred, and clearly they must be given priority in any consideration of the circumstances in which songs would be transmitted. Certain public houses in Navy towns created the same situation in miniature.

It would, however, be taking an extreme romantic or idealistic view to imagine that authentic traditional Navy songs were sung one after another all evening without a break. Like most folk songs they made their appearance interspersed with sentimental ballads, popular songs from the music halls and later from the top ten, plus the general Service/rugger club type of offerings.

Even under these casual circumstances, the presence of a piano, perhaps on a small platform, and sometimes with a self-appointed Master of Ceremonies emerging to administer some measure of control, lent a small degree of near-formality to the occasion, compared, that is, to the sing-songs that might start up at any time and in any venue round a table. No music was needed here, and neither was there any need for an MC.

Another setting for the dissemination of songs was a form of smoking concert, an all-male affair known in the RN as a 'Sod's

Opera'. The principal difference between Sod's Operas and the normal canteen-type sing-song was that they tended to be more organised. They were usually announced in advance and were often planned a little more, with contributors singing according to a prearranged order, though this was not always the case, a measure of spontaneity being understood as a necessary ingredient. Furthermore, Sod's Operas were as often as not held on board ship and served as a safety-valve for crews who had been deprived of shore entertainment too long for their own good. There was no need on these occasions for any rules of censorship (nor was there usually in the canteen environment) and in consequence ribaldry could be given free rein. The Sod's Opera was an ideal time to bring out the true Navy song whether ribald or not, and it is likely that many of these would be aired during the evening.

In addition to Sod's Operas there were more formal ship's concerts. The audience at such productions might include anyone; leading civic dignitaries from neighbouring towns, wives, girl friends or daughters of officers or men, as well as the senior officers of ships in company. They were, therefore, much more respectable affairs than Sod's Operas. Whether or not a true RN song ever found its way into the evening's entertainment is not easy to deduce. No informant mentioned these formal ship's concerts as the source of their songs, and I have examined many programmes listing the items performed at these functions without ever coming across any evidence that traditional RN items of any kind were included.

Informal singing on board ship, by an individual or a small group of men would be possible either at work or during leisure hours, but this needs more investigation. Certainly the 'dhoby session', when ratings would gather in the washroom to do their laundry by hand, was one occasion when song-swapping was habitual, and at least one song, 'Onward Christian Sailors' (No. 22), grew out of this specific ship-board situation.

Establishing the degree to which sailors sang while at their work is not easy. Circumstances varied from ship to ship, and from job to job. Where there was no threat to efficiency there would probably be no restriction imposed, but that is still not to say that Jack broke into song very often. The 'Paint Ship' songs (Nos 5 and 6) were certainly sung by ratings as they dangled over the ship's side and elsewhere, but I doubt whether the toilers in the colliers and bunkers had any breath to spare for singing the 'Coal Ship' songs (Nos 2, 3 and 4) at their work, quite apart from the fact that a band, either Royal Marines or an improvised ensemble from among the ship's company, usually kept up a constant accompaniment to their labours.

But irrespective of whether or not the twentieth-century matelot sang much at his work, an examination of the respective sections in this book will soon reveal that, as subjects for song-making, work and ship's routine were in his mind quite as much as the joys of shore life, a fact which more than meets Captain Whall's challenge 'Where, then, is the theme for song?'

In the Steamship Navy songs served only one purpose, that of diversion or entertainment. My father, though, recalled that on one of his messdecks, should a member begin discussing some aspect of work when the rest were trying to enjoy a bit of leisure, his messmates would begin to pound the table and chant:

> Leave the ship in the water,
> Leave the ship in the water,
> Leave the ship in the water,
> And don't bring the bastard down here.

The tune was very basic, and the simple chorus can hardly be described as a song, but we have here an isolated example of singing serving a purpose other than recreational.

In earlier days there had been another reason for singing, and special songs called shanties were reserved for this purpose. Due to the confusion that has arisen in modern times from the careless use of this term to include any song with a nautical flavour it will be as well to point out that the shanty was a song only to be found on sailing-ships, because it was a work-song harnessed to specific tasks aboard such vessels. It was used to unify the collected efforts of a number of men engaged in the same work, for greater efficiency, together with a secondary function of making that work a little less irksome. Once steam replaced sail these tasks, and consequently these needs, disappeared and the shanty fell into disuse. This is not to say that some shanties did not continue to be sung as social songs (as they are today in folk clubs), but, from the moment steam displaced sail, there was thenceforth only one reason for singing, not two. The shanty, insofar as it was purely a work-song, ceased to exist.

Furthermore, although there is evidence to refute the oft-repeated nonsense that shantying was strictly forbidden in the Royal Navy, or that only two specific shanties were permitted, it is undoubtedly true that the practice was rare in the Royal service and was almost wholly confined to merchantmen. In spite of all the technical advances, though, there have always been certain tasks on a warship which could have been helped with a work-song: loading torpedoes into the fore-ends of a conventional submarine for instance. Instead the sailor makes do with chants such as 'two-six, HEAVE!' On the other hand when William Cole accuses today's Jack Tar of being unable to 'tell a shanty from a shoehorn' I do not think this is what he had in mind. Rather, as in the BBC phrase, 'Brain of Britain' alliteration has been allowed to triumph over terminological accuracy, and Mr Cole is really referring to sea songs in general.

We are told that one reason shantying was discouraged in the old-time Royal Navy was that it constituted a threat to discipline. Out of earshot of the officers it would be possible for the shantyman to improvise lines reviling or criticising his superiors or the Service itself for the amusement of his fellows. In the first half of the twentieth century compulsory church attendance presented the bluejacket with a similar opportunity. Any chaplain or commanding officer who really believed that the men in the rearmost rows were singing the orthodox texts printed on the hymn-sheets would have been too naive for words. Hymn tunes provided Jack with one of his favourite vehicles for carrying the fruits of his imagination. With men dragooned into an Act of Worship as these were, church services were apt to seem even more tedious than they might otherwise have been, and any ploy was welcome that helped to inject a little zest into the proceedings and made the time pass more agreeably. When the chaplain's sonorous tones boomed out 'The sea is His' a sharp ear could hardly fail to detect the answering murmur 'and He can have it.'

It has to be remembered that ordinary sailors were the people who had to 'rig church', and later unrig it, which in a way was rubbing salt into the wound. As there were still facilities for raising the anchor by hand in the event of a power failure, a simple way to improvise pews was to upturn wooden buckets and pass capstan-bars through their rope handles. No wonder Jack was often heard singing:

'The church's one foundation is capstan-bars and buckets.'

A later generation sang 'capstans, spars and buckets', a garbled form which made no real sense.

Mention has been made of authentic Navy songs making their

appearance side by side with other categories of song during evenings in the fleet canteens or other singing venues. The collector has few problems in segregating sentimental ballads and popular songs, except for one or two of the older music-hall songs on Naval subjects which a little research can usually identify. But in the rugger song department it is sometimes made more difficult by the content of the song and by the fact that such content leads the average sailor himself to vow the song is a genuine RN product. Sophisticated bawdy pieces like 'The Good Ship *Venus*' do not, however, come across as sailor-made songs, and I am inclined to think they are more likely to be the product of higher education, having their origins in universities or medical colleges. After-match rugger sing-songs could account for them finding their way on to the Navy messdecks, although it must be borne in mind that the 1939-45 war, followed by post-war National Service, introduced a transitory academic element into the lower-deck community. (In compiling the Glossary I was struck by the almost total absence of Navy slang in the 'War' section.) Placed side by side with the songs in this collection these slick rugger items stick out like sore thumbs, amusing though they may be. What serves to confuse matters is that Jack will gleefully *adopt* the pornographic song when he encounters it, and is quite adept at making ribald adornments to any existing song. Yet the evidence suggests that he makes up fewer obscene songs himself than is generally supposed. Quite contrary to popular belief the overwhelming majority of songs *originating* in the Royal Navy would hardly shock a maiden aunt.

Since 1945 radical changes have taken place in the Royal Navy which may have had a detrimental effect on singing and songmaking in the Service. They can be summed up as follows. First capital ships have disappeared, giving way to ships mostly of the equivalent size, though of course not strike power, of the old destroyer. This has reduced the size of the typical floating community, and with it, theoretically, the quantity of possible available talent in the singing/song-making line likely to be on board any given ship. It could also be postulated that large ships produced a greater sense of anonymity in the individual, which found expression in song (see 'Roll on the Aeroplane Navy', No. 74).

Second, the number of ships has been greatly reduced so that the number of floating communities at any given time is much smaller.

9

Thus there no longer take place the vast canteen get-togethers that were witnessed at places like Scapa Flow and Invergordon, where thousands of sailors who had entered port almost simultaneously, especially after fleet exercises, would surge ashore on the same evening to let off steam. Besides affecting the actual incidence of singing, this factor would also hamper the process of oral transmission of songs, since there are bound to be far fewer people listening to the performance of a given song at any one time.

Third, the length of tour of duty away from home, called in the Royal Navy 'foreign commissions', has been considerably reduced. There is in consequence less time for the men on board a given ship to weld themselves together as a homogeneous community. If it is true that the incidence of song-making is in any way related to the degree of integration of the enclosed community concerned, then this must be considered an adverse development, in this one respect at any rate.

Fourth, like most other British communities a ship's company is much less dependent on its own resources for providing entertainment than was the case before 1945. Film-shows, radio and, in home waters, television, as well as tape recorders and cassette-players have all proliferated, bringing the effects of mass entertainment more and more into the daily lives of those at sea and reducing the necessity of home-made amusement. However, too much should not be made of this point. From the moment the gramophone record became a commercial proposition it played its role in ship-board entertainment. From the evidence of a diary of my father's, kept whilst in the cruiser *Durban* in South American waters around 1931–2, it seems he was the ship's 'disc-jockey', probably by virtue of his place of work being the wireless office. Every day he made an entry such as 'Gram. 2½ hrs.', or 'Gram. 1 hr.', presumably to be able to claim some remuneration. This suggests that by the 1930s the entertainment media were already making their presence felt, yet the collected songs from that period give abundant evidence that song-making was flourishing as much as ever.

Fifth, singing ashore has declined. There are several reasons for this, I believe: (a) For the same reason that the civilian population find it increasingly difficult to sing in pubs, so does the sailor, namely the almost universal presence of the juke-box or live amplified music. The latter may possibly be avoided by removing oneself to another room (if one can be found in today's unicameral brewery world), but the juke-box is usually a 'big brother' with extension speakers in every bar.

(b) The removal of the necessity for RN personnel to wear uniform ashore seems to have produced inhibitions that previously did not exist. It is as if the airing of the songs had been inextricably bound up with the mode of dress of the performers, and that the singing of Navy songs whilst wearing clothes associated with civilian life was an incongruity. To this limited extent William Cole's observations are pertinent.

(c) There has been a considerable increase in the amount of weekend leave allowed to RN personnel. Fifty or sixty years ago a sailor would only rarely see his family between periods of 'long leave' unless they lived near his naval base. Even after 1945 a 'long weekend' lasting from tea-time on Friday until first thing Monday morning was a carefully-rationed privilege, a sailor being perhaps entitled to only one or two between periods of long leave. Uniformed men were therefore to be found in profusion in the naval ports at weekends, which, coming as they did close after pay-day, were the favourite occasions for celebrating ashore. It is more common these days, however, for the sailor to be free for a long weekend any time he is not required for duty. Furthermore these long weekends have grown longer, lasting, say, from Friday forenoon until 'first train Monday'. This, coupled with faster inter-city rail services guarantees even those men with homes at the other end of the country two clear days with their families. The inevitable result is that far fewer sailors are now to be found footloose in a naval port at weekends. Those who have not travelled home or perhaps just 'up the line' to London are for the most part either duty on board or 'natives' domiciled in the port area, neither of which categories can be considered as potential participants in a Navy sing-song in those few city centre pubs where such a thing is still possible.

(d) A further factor not unrelated to (a) is that a new kind of landlord has taken the place of the old-style publican. Often young and ambitious, anxious to make his way in the licensed trade as rapidly as possible, and frequently a manager under the dominance of the brewery and its notions, he is totally out of sympathy with anything that does not reflect the latest ideas in public house management. The concept of informal, spontaneous singing on his premises is something which, to him, went out with spit and sawdust (there persists in England a moral correlation between 'unorganised' singing and drunkenness), and he is likely to stifle at its outset any attempt to compete with the musical amenities he himself has provided. Moreover the changes indicated above have led to a diminution of the sailor's importance as a source of trade in comparison with the civilian population, with a consequent decrease in the dependence on Jack and an associated lessening of sympathy with Jack's ways. The old-time landlord was well aware that sailors meant money and would seldom be foolish enough to suppress a song session that was bound to be good for business.

It is unnecessary, I am sure, to stress that in reducing the actual incidence of singing in the Royal Navy the foregoing factors must at the same time be adversely affecting the oral circulation of existing songs and fresh compositions, and drawing on such considerations alone we might justifiably conclude that if the harvesting of the songs to follow has been for me a lengthy and uphill business such a collection may be doubly so in twenty or thirty years time.

Fortunately all change has not been for the worse. Since the late 1950s there has been one significant development that has taken place in Britain which may on its own cancel out much of the damage effected by the various transitions described above. I refer to the Folk Song Revival. Folk song clubs have now existed in nearly every town and city, and in many villages too, for a great many years. Although much of the material heard in them is old and traditional the audience is made up mostly of young people who have by now left their elders completely behind in the matter of familiarity with the traditional heritage of music and song. It is no exaggeration to describe the movement as 'underground'. Any phenomenon of which so many of the public and the media too can remain so unaware while it flourishes under their very noses deserves no other label.

What significance has this folk song movement in respect of Royal Navy song? At the time I took my discharge in May 1959 I regarded myself as possibly the only person in the Service whose hobby was folk song. Yet within ten years the folk song habit had spread to every Naval port area, with several clubs to choose from not only in each town but actually in many Royal Naval establishments themselves. One reason for this folk renaissance in the Senior Service could have been that for the first time in its history the Royal Navy, thanks to the folk club movement, was recruiting youngsters some of whom were going into uniform with a more highly developed awareness of traditional song, old sailing-ship songs and shanties among them, than any of the veteran serving men. They had been listening to them every week back home, perhaps since they left school. What more natural than that they should wish to continue with their pastime after they had enlisted? Moreover the folk movement had given rise to a considerable amount of recorded performances of British folk song performed in a relatively authentic manner, again including nautical material, and these youngsters were bringing their records with them. The important effect of all this is that, willingly or not, hundreds more sailors year by year have been exposed to, and in many cases have become addicted to, the old-style sailor song, so that when they in their turn have come to express themselves in song, as many seem now to be doing, they are likely to be influenced as much by the old idiom as they are by current trends in pop music.

And still, despite Captain Whall's despair, there is no dearth of themes. The stoppage of the rum issue produced several offerings. As to the general standard, the individual compositions that have emanated from the Royal Navy in the past couple of decades are of a quality that encourages the highest optimism for the future of song in the Senior Service. It may even be entering upon its finest period.

THE SONGS

SHIP'S ROUTINE

Sea songs in general are songs referring to the sea. They are rarely sung by the sailors themselves.

R. DUNSTAN in *Musical Appreciation Through Song*, Huddersfield, 1933

How true. Much has been said about the futility of attempts by well-meaning outsiders to write songs on behalf of communities to which they do not belong, and in the past the sailor has never gone short of unsolicited offerings of this kind. But, as Dr Dunstan says, they rarely found a place in the sailor's repertoire. This was because, with a few exceptions, such as Eliza Cook's 'The Sailor's Grave', their sentiments were utterly at variance with those of the people about whom they were written.

At the very least the landlubber writing cheery ballads in praise of the seaman's life ought first to ensure he has good sea-legs himself if he wishes to avoid social embarrassment. Bryan Waller Proctor (Barry Cornwall), dying a thousand deaths on a Channel crossing, had also to endure the callous humour of his wife who, hale and hearty, marched up and down the deck in front of him humming the refrain of one of his own songs, the words of which assured everyone that:

> I'm on the sea, I'm on the sea!
> I am where I would ever be,
> With the blue above and the blue below,
> And silence wheresoe'er I go.
> If a storm should come and awake the deep,
> What matter? What matter? I shall ride and sleep.

The twentieth century has, thankfully, seen a rapid decline in such idealised nonsense, probably because far less romance is attached to steel and steam than to timber and sail. Consequently the field has been left almost entirely to the matelot himself, with the result that those wishing to know what life has really been like on board a man-o'-war in modern times are far less likely to be misled than were their Victorian counterparts. The sailor puts his songs together from first-hand experience and pulls no punches. Compare Barry Cornwall's lines above with the third verse of the following:

1 *That's what it's like in the Navy*
(Tune: See Appendix D)

I wish I'd never joined for a sailor, mother dear,
I've seen some places in my time, but nothing like this 'ere,
The girls won't let us court them and the canteen's out of beer,
And that's what it's like in the Navy.

They covered us with honours, and praises far from faint,
They showered us with medals, 'gainst which we've no complaint,
But we'd rather that our 'Jimmy' hadn't covered us with paint,
And that's what it's like in the Navy.

And when we started rolling, we rolled an awful lot,
Some people lost their balance, or their dinner, on the spot,
But the whole of bloody Two Mess went and lost their soddin' tot,
And that's what it's like in the Navy.

There were tough guys in the Navy when Francis banged his drum,
And chaps like Hawkins chewed up glass instead of chewing gum,
But even they weren't tough enough to drink Maltese water in their
    rum,
And that's what it's like in the Navy.

For the sake of present-day Maltese tourism perhaps I should point out that the above song shows its age in the last verse. From personal experience I can say that today the island's water supply is as good as anywhere else!

Lower-deck lyrics are not only straight from the shoulder, they can be admirably succinct into the bargain. When S. J. Arnold penned the words of 'A Life on the Ocean Wave' in 1838 he can hardly have anticipated Jack's broadside of an answer a few generations later, and the point it has taken this present writer some 300 words to make is pungently summarised by the sailor himself in those eight short lines:

2 Coal Ship Song (I)
(Tune: 'A Life on the Ocean Wave')

A Life on the Ocean Wave,
The fellow that wrote that song,
I'd like to shit on his grave
A turd about nine inches long.
'Cos he's never been to sea
On a Sunday afternoon,
And he's never coaled ship in his watch below
Or he'd bloody soon change his tune . . .

In civilian life even the humblest wage-slave could take a stand on the right to some sort of respite from their labours but, if the needs of the Service so decreed, the bluejacket was entitled to nothing. If it meant 'turning to' on the Sabbath, his one day of rest, then so be it, and, as was pointed out in a *Hampshire Telegraph* article in 1959, when it came to 'coaling ship' it was not just the rank-and-file lower-deck personnel who were dragooned into this squalid but vital operation:

> In the days of coal-burning ships in the Royal Navy, 'coal ship' day was a major operation in which every officer and rating of the ship's company, including the chaplain, but excluding the commander and surgeon, took part. In November 1908 I joined HMS *Prince of Wales* to serve in the newly-formed Atlantic Fleet. . . . She had just returned to Gibraltar and, in consequence, the day after it was 'coal ship' day. Her usual intake was about 2,000 tons. The whole of this coal had to be shovelled from the collier alongside into baskets (sacks in home ports), hoisted up, and the baskets or sacks carried to the shutes leading down to the bunkers. There was always keen competition between the ships of the Navy to achieve the record in completing 'coal ship' and, on November 1st 1909, we made a world's record by taking in an average of 329.8 tons per hour.

Needless to say, with so much coal and dust flying around, everything and everyone – boiler suits were not issued then – was covered in grime. Yet directly the coal was in all hands proceeded to wash down the ship inside and out, and within a few hours she was as clean as a new pin.

(M. J. Golightly)

And, as the song says, all this could take place during your 'watch below' or off-duty period! No wonder there is no shortage of songs on the subject, the most widespread being:

3 Coal Ship Song (II)
(Tune: 'Holy, Holy, Holy' with 'Loch Lomond' interpolated)

Coaling, coaling, coaling,
Always bloody well coaling,
Coaling in the morning and coaling half the night.
Coaling, coaling, coaling,
It may be first thing Monday morning

'Always bloody well coaling'

20

Or last thing Saturday night,
Always bloody well coaling.
You hold the bag and I'll shovel up,
And we'll both go to coal ship together.
When the collier comes along
We'll sing this little song:
Coaling, coaling, coaling,
Always bloody well coaling,
It's a good job we didn't join for ever.

Nothing could be more appealing to the poor work-weary sailor than the prospect of being released from this drudgery, and sometimes he adapted the foregoing song to:

Coaling, coaling, coaling,
Always bloody well coaling,
Send me back to Barracks
And I will coal no more.

which in its turn was transformed into the messdeck slogan:

Roll on my five,
Then I will coal no more.

Another song which made much the same point as 'Coaling, coaling, coaling' but which, for reasons of scansion and rhyme, must have been restricted to one particular ship was:

4 *Coal Ship Song (III)*
(Tune: 'In the Good Old Summertime')

In the good old cruiser *Kent*,
In the good old cruiser *Kent*,
Coaling ship three times a week
Till all our energy's spent.
We never wash our coaling rig,
And very good reason for why,
We'd be coaling ship again
Before we could get them dry.

21

Even when the ship had been duly washed down it might be found necessary to apply a fresh coat of paint. In any case, whether in coal-burners or not, very little excuse was necessary for this operation, as Godfrey Winn points out in *P.Q. 17* (Hutchinson, 1947):

> There is one practice in all navies which never deviates throughout the seven seas. When in idleness, when in doubt, the command goes forth: paint ship. It doesn't matter how short a time back a whole coating was applied, repeat the process and go on repeating it; the sides, the superstructure, the woodwork on the upper deck; paint the same stanchions over and over again rather than that the men should be idle with time on their hands, to loaf, in working hours.

On these occasions the 'Loch Lomond' segment of 'Coaling, coaling, coaling' was suitably adapted to a form which remains in circulation to the present day:

'You take the paint pot
And I'll take the brush'

22

5 *Paint Ship Song (I)*
(Tune: 'Loch Lomond')

You take the paint pot
And I'll take the brush,
And we'll paint the ship's side together.
When 'Jimmy' comes along
We'll sing this little song:
Thank the lord we didn't join for ever.

Another song on the same subject was sung on board HMS *Stuart*, Second Destroyer Flotilla, in 1929–31, and no doubt on many other ships as well. It parodied a hit song published in 1929:

6 *Paint Ship Song (II)*
(Tune: 'Just Plain Folk')

Just grey paint, just grey paint,
We know where the paint comes from,
Underneath the old pom-pom.
Just grey paint,
Makes things look what they ain't.
'Jimmy' goes sick when he looks at the chit
For just grey paint.

As will be gathered from these 'paint ship' songs, the general appearance of a Royal Navy vessel, her paintwork, cleanliness and overall smartness, was the direct responsibility of the First Lieutenant, otherwise known as 'Jimmy the One' or simply 'Jimmy'. But while an over-zealous first lieutenant might earn unstinted praise in wardroom circles there could be a price to pay in terms of lower-deck morale:

7 *She's a Tiddley Ship*
(Tune: See Appendix D)

She's a tiddley ship, through the ocean she'll flip,
She's sailing by night and by day,

And when she's in motion she's the pride of the ocean,
You can't see her stern-sheets for spray.
On the side, side, *Ariadne*'s ship's side,
And 'Jimmy' looks on her with pride.
He throws a pink fit if he sees any shit
On the side of *Ariadne*'s ship's side.

Chorus
This is my story, this is my song,
We've been in commission too bloody long.
Roll on the *Nelson*, the *Rodney, Renown*,
This four-funnelled bastard is getting me down.

or:

Roll on the *Nelson*, the *Rodney*, the *Hood*,
This four-funnelled bastard is no bleeding good.

'Tiddley Ship' must be one of the best (and best known) anti-bull songs to emerge since the nineteenth-century Jack Tar bemoaned his spit-and-polish existence on board the old *La Pique*. But whereas that song was about one ship and one ship only, our twentieth-century offering is to be found adapted to whatever vessel the singer chooses, usually the one he's serving on at the time. The chorus parodies the hymn 'Blessed Assurance', and the last two lines give a good idea of the song's age. Presumably the capital ships mentioned had yet to be commissioned, which would date it from the years immediately following the First World War, although the term 'roll on' could merely evince a desire to be drafted to one of the ships in question, in which case the song could date from the 1920s or, less likely, the 1930s. The advent of the battleships named promised the very latest in comfortable shipboard living and, who could tell, perhaps a more liberal, flannel-free routine to go with it. As time went on the number of funnels in the last line was reduced to three, two or one. The word 'bastard' was sometimes softened to the equally apt 'bathtub', and it is interesting to compare line 7 of the verse with line 6 of 'Just Grey Paint'. In the one we have 'Jimmy' going berserk at the paintwork being spoiled, in the other he is anxious about the actual expense of painting ship, but the two lines seem clearly related, which invites speculation as to which came first. The probability is that 'Tiddley Ship' pre-dates 'Just Grey Paint' by a few years.

From 1941 onwards a tasteless substitution for the whole of the last line was heard to creep in occasionally:

You can't have the *Hood* 'cos the bastard's gone down.

I have been given this line by numerous individuals, but under what circumstances anyone would risk singing it to a gathering of wartime RN personnel I find it hard to imagine. It is reassuring to note that the more orthodox last line still prevails among present-day sailors and, even more surprising, the third line of the chorus seems to have remained unaffected by the passing away of the capital ships concerned. Jack still sings 'Roll on the Nelson', etc.

Most probably the frequency with which ships needed painting decreased with the phasing-out of the coal-burners, and no doubt the seaman's sense of frustration was correspondingly assuaged. He was now able to admire his handiwork for a more reasonable length of time before being called upon to repeat the process. There were certain 'parts of ship', however, where the struggle to contain the inevitable defilement attendant upon day-to-day human usage remained a never-ending chore, and nowhere more so than in the toilets, or 'heads'. Perhaps as some form of compensation, the unfortunate person who found this his sphere of activity was unofficially referred to as 'Captain of the Heads'.

8 Captain of the Heads' Lament
(Tune: 'Begin the Beguine')

My job is to clean a naval latrine,
I'm the man with the plan for the pan that everyone uses,
The paper's OK – on both sides the news is,
You know what I mean, in my latrine.
I clean it by night, and I clean it by day,
I keep it the way, the way you'd expect it,
And when it gets high I just disinfect it,
Terrifically clean is my latrine.
I clean it by day, and at four in the morning,
My oppo joins in, we polish the chains,
And there we are scrubbing away together,

25

'My job is to clean a naval latrine'

Wondering if ever we'll get out the stains.
What joys we have seen, what raptures we've tasted,
Then along comes the gang, and we know our efforts were wasted.
They shit anywhere, they don't care where they place it,
It fair makes you scream, in my latrine.

26

I've laid traps for the chaps who have craps in all directions,
I've even laid grass for each arse to establish connections,
But I stay aloof,
They can't reach the roof,
That's one place that's clean, in my latrine.

For a traditional piece this is untypically sophisticated, but there is ample proof that it has been in oral circulation, though to get the best effect a canteen pianist is a useful asset.

Any member of a ship's company could suffer at the hands of an over-keen superior, and it wasn't just 'Jimmy' that the songsters had a go at. It might be the coxswain, 'buffer', 'jaunty', or even the Captain himself:

9 *Swim Back you Bastard to Me*
(Tune: 'My Bonny Lies Over the Ocean')

If the skipper fell into the oggin,
If the skipper fell into the sea,
If the skipper fell into the oggin,
He'd get sod-all lifebelt from me.

Chorus
Swim back, swim back,
Oh swim back you bastard to me, to me,
Swim back, swim back,
Oh swim back you bastard to me.

Any suitable two-syllable personage could be substituted for 'skipper'.

If anyone did fall into the 'oggin', or sea, there were usually enough boats available to go to the rescue. When the ship was at anchor they spent much of the time attached to booms projecting from the ship's side, and it often seemed that what with mooring and unmooring, cleaning and maintenance the boats' crews, too, spent most of their working day 'out on a limb' as it were:

10 *On the Booms*
(Tune: See Appendix D)

Oh the coxswain of the launch he didn't stand a chance
On the booms, on the booms,
And the coxswain of the pinnace he didn't quite finish
On the booms, on the booms.

Oh the coxswain of the cutter he didn't stop to fuck her
On the booms, on the booms,
And the coxswain of the whaler he was up another sailor
On the booms, on the booms.

Oh the coxswain of the galley he didn't stop to dally
On the booms, on the booms,
And the coxswain of the skiff well he didn't get a sniff
On the booms, on the booms.

A simple challenge to the matelot's rhyming ingenuity. In line one, 'launch' would be pronounced 'lahnch'.

'On the booms'

No one envied people in such exposed places when the weather was bitterly cold and wet, and in the days when soundings were taken by lead-line an even less coveted duty was to stand in 'the chains', the small projecting platform from where the leadsman cast his line. No shelter from the wintry blast and lashing rain here. The leadsman's calls to the Captain, Navigator or Officer-of-the-Watch were often inaudible against a gale and had to be repeated, which gave rise to a piece of foolery indulged in during my father's time in the Service. Where a depth reading involved a half-fathom the word 'half' was called out before the whole number. While the latter was heavily stressed, the 'half' was called in a high, sustained intonation, thus:

'And a HA-A-ALF *six*, sir!'

With the freezing wet line running through his numb hands and the gale whipping his face, the leadsman would sometimes call out his own 'reading' of the depth:

Leadsman: 'It ain't HA-A-ALF *cold*, sir!'
OOW: 'Say again, leadsman.'
Leadsman: 'And a HA-A-LF *five*, sir!'

If the leadsman was inexperienced, to add to his discomfort there was always the danger of over-swinging the lead and having it strike him on the head. All in all, the leadsman's lot was far from happy, and many were the times he must have prayed for the end of his spell of duty, especially if it was the forenoon watch and warming grog and dinner beckoned:

11 *The Leadsman's Lament*
(Tune: Probably 'Oh Lord of Heaven and Earth')

Oh Lord, when I am in the chains,
Stop me from knocking out my brains,
Send me an oilskin when it rains,
And a smart relief.

For sad and weary is my lot.
Some lousy bastard's drunk my tot
I'll go below and swipe the lot.
I'll show them all.

We have seen that the leadsmen and the seaboats' crews between them endured what was probably the bleakest existence of the whole ship's company, but these weren't specialist jobs. At different times one man could find himself assigned to both tasks, and another mock-prayer neatly ties the two together, as well as echoing the previous lament:

12 To the Man in the Chains

To the man in the chains
Send an oilskin when it rains,
And if it pleases You
Take me from the seaboat's crew.

The longing for a 'smart relief' in 'The Leadsman's Lament' focuses on a very sensitive area of personal relationships, both in the Royal Navy and out of it. 'Smart' here means 'prompt', and to relieve the previous watchkeeper late was regarded as a cardinal offence against propriety. Conversely, the man who turned up early for the start of his watch was likely to be held in high esteem. The end of a watch coincided with the ringing of the hour on the ship's bell by the quartermaster who, on larger ships in former days, was usually a Royal Marine, or 'bootneck':

13 Sammy Ring the Bell
(Tune: See Appendix D)

Sammy ring the bell,
Sammy ring the bell,
Four hours on watch is a bloody long spell.
Cold, hard and hungry,
Bloody nigh dead as well.
Ring, you rubber-necked, bootneck bastard,
Ring that bloody bell!

Considering the long-standing rivalry and good-humoured leg-pulling traditional between the Royal Navy and the Royal Marines

30

there seem to be surprisingly few songs which deal with this aspect, and 'Sammy Ring the Bell' must be regarded as a rarity.

The ringing of the ship's bell may have served its purpose adequately enough on the upper deck, but down in the bowels of the ship, amid the boiler-tubes and furnaces, the clock was the sole arbiter. The following snippets, possibly belonging to longer songs, furnish brief glimpses into this sweating world of wheel-spanners, gauges and oily cotton-waste:

14 *Chiefy Loves Me*
(Tune: 'Jesus Loves Me')

Chiefy loves me, this I know
'Cos the watchbill tells me so.
I've the middle watch to keep
While me mates is fast asleep.

•

15 *Orders Came for Sailing*
(Tune: 'Lili Marlene')

Orders came for sailing, flash up number one,
Go and chase up Chiefy, the panic has begun.
Tiffies are rushing here and there,
It's hot down here, but the pigs don't care.
We're flashing up regardless,
We've got to go to sea.

16 *The Stoker's Complaint*
(Tune: 'The Mountains of Mourne')

There are men in the Navy are known as POs,
But what they are there for, the lord only knows.
They stand on the plates and they bawl and they shout,
And order the poor old King's Dustmen about.

'Chiefy' signifies either the Chief Engine Room Artificer (CERA) or

'We're flashing up regardless,
We've got to go to sea'

Chief Stoker. While the former was a senior artificer, the latter was responsible for the remainder of the engine room personnel, the stokers, and in the old coal-burning ships this meant that he reigned supreme in the stokehold:

17 *The Stoker's Lament*
(*Tune: 'Villikins and his Dinah'*)

Down in the stokehold there's all sorts of jobs,
Priming and topping and sorting out cobs.
'Oh Chiefy, oh Chiefy, there's none here,' I cried.
'Well you'll bleeding soon find some if I hop inside!'

Chorus
Hold yer row, what d'ye say?
We'll shag all Chief Stokers who come down our way.

Now we've got a Chief Stoker who's not very tall,
He comes down and shakes us and gives us a call.
'Come on now, me hearties, get lashed up and stow,
'Get yer bleeding breakfast and get down below.'

Down in the stokehold, it's not very deep,
A second class stoker is having a sleep.
Don't shake him, oh Chiefy, but just let him rest,
For that second class stoker's been doing his best.

Royal Naval Artificers were sometimes referred to as 'the gentlemen of the lower deck', not so much because of their demeanour or diction, but more by virtue of their generally superior level of education, their arduous four-year training period, and their extra rate of pay. Unlike other members of the ship's company they had the comfort of knowing that NCO status was theirs by right. Having once reached the level of Petty Officer they could not be demoted below it, as other ratings could. On the other hand they had to face the fact that, with the exception of the most senior CERA, their rank did not carry quite the same 'pull' as that of their equivalents in most other branches, and bore no corresponding promise of an easier life supervising the efforts of others. They were, nevertheless, objects of jealousy, and jibes at their expense were, perhaps, less good-natured than those directed at, for instance, the Royal Marines. Whether the next song was one such or was made up from within the ranks of the 'tiffies' themselves is anyone's guess:

18 *The Ragtime Tiffy*

He's a ragtime tiffy, ragtime tiffy,
Early every morning with a spanner in his hands,
Walking round the engine room tightening up the glands,
He's a ragtime tiffy, ragtime tiffy,
Happy as the flowers in May,
But if you ask him what the bloody hell he's doing
He don't know what the bloody hell to say.

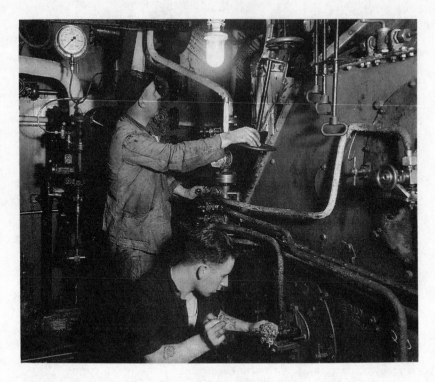

'He's a ragtime tiffy'

Further down still perhaps, especially if the ship had sprung a leak, one might come across the Shipwright, or ship's carpenter, popularly known as 'Chippy', trying his best to make her watertight again and usually succeeding, even if he had to work all night as well as day. A brand-new ship was seldom snag-free, and if RN personnel were entitled to overtime pay there would often have been a fortune to be made on 'shake-down' cruises. But at least their labours carried with them the consolation that by the law of averages everything would turn out right in the end. For the crews of old and leaky ships, perhaps only a couple of commissions away from the breaker's yard, there was no such comfort. They were fighting a losing battle with the wear and tear of time and they knew it. As usual, though, humour came to the rescue:

34

19 Corrosion has Set In
(Tune: 'Dahn Below')

Corrosion has set in
Dahn below.
The plates are getting thin
Dahn below.
There's a leak in the fore peak,
And how those bulkheads creak,
I hope we'll last the week
Dahn below.

Boiler room's a-leaking
Dahn below.
Crack is nicely seeping
Dahn below.
Fire and bilge will do their best
While the diver's getting dressed,
Splinter-box will do the rest
Dahn below.

Chippy wears a frahn
Dahn below.
It's coming in again
Dahn below.
They've taken up a shore
To the for'ard naval store
And they're sawing up some more
Dahn below.

Chippy's got an ulcer
Dahn below.
It plays him up a treat
Dahn below.
His feet are getting wet
As he watches concrete set,
But he's short of 'aggreget'
Dahn below.

The ship is like a sieve
Dahn below.

I hope they're PST
Dahn below.
For the lifeboats they inflate
Premature. Can this be fate?
Oh we're in a ghastly state
Dahn below.

An examination of this collection should soon reveal that naval humour comes in two distinct forms. On the one hand there is, as in the foregoing song, humour based on reality, or at least on recognised possibilities. Exaggerations there may be, but they usually refer to a state of affairs that could occur. On the other hand we have humour amounting to sheer fantasy, dealing with the utterly bizarre and impossible, and the next song demonstrates how the same predicament, a ship falling to pieces, can lead Jack's imagination into the zaniest realms.

I first discovered that there was a Royal Navy song along these lines whilst talking to a morris dancer at Sidmouth Folk Festival in 1962. He could recall no more than the chorus and a few lines, and at first I thought I was listening to a straightforward parody of the East Coast song 'The Collier Brig', Bob Roberts's 1960 recording of which might easily have found its way on to some messdeck or other. However, when the singer informed me that he had been many years out of the Navy and had never heard of 'The Collier Brig' it seemed evident that somewhere or other there was a matelot's version with a distinct life of its own. Eventually, after over five years of searching, I received in December 1967 the set of words printed here. My informant had lost his original copy and qualified the accuracy of his text as follows:

I've written down some stanzas in a reasonable semblance of order from memory. Actually they're probably just the same because I wrote down the words from memory in the first place, a couple of days after I actually heard them. The singer was an unknown Leading Seaman and the chorus was a half dozen of his oppos. The place was Corradino Canteen, Malta, 1963, and the setting very beery! There's at least one verse I know is missing and there's maybe two. I think the song was originally about HMS *Chilcompton*, a 'ton'-class minesweeper, but it could really apply to any ship, depending on just how vicious the singer feels.

20 *Waiting for the Day*
(Tune: Based on 'Another Little Drink Won't Do Us Any Harm')
(Repeat for chorus)

Oh the crabbiest ship the Yard's ever laid
Steamed out of Plymouth on a Winter's day

Chorus:
And we're waiting for the day, waiting for the day,
Waiting for the day that we get our pay.

She was laid down in Nelson's time,
Held together with seaming twine

Her keel is buckled and the rudder won't turn
She's steered by a dhoby-bucket hung on the stern

The skipper's queer and the Jimmy's a Jew
Watch on deck ten men too few

The Engineer's pissed and so is the 'Swain
They've been at the FFO again

Even the victualling's all to cock
We've a ton of corned dog from Devonport Dock

We reached Grand Harbour in the month of May
When we met with a di-so in Bighi Bay

Well the lashings parted and the bottom fell out
There was four dozen matelots swimming all about

If there hadn't been so much tickler to save
We all would've met with a watery grave

Now the moral of this story's easy to tell
For we're in the NAAFI but the skipper's in Hell

So gather round boys and remember the name
On a 'ton'-class sweeper we sank to fame

FFO: Furnace fuel oil. Not used on such minesweepers, which ran on diesel fuel oil, suggesting that the song was carried to *Chilcompton* from another ship.

There may or may not be a connection between the Sidmouth version and the Malta version. Whether the latter was modelled on 'The Collier Brig' (there are several points of similarity) or on some traditional RN version (there are many purely 'pusser' stanzas) is hard to decide on the evidence available at the moment. Either way it is a prime example of the bluejacket's gift for outlandish imagery.

To return to the serious, realistic aspect of a ship taking in water dangerously, in the past many vessels must have been lost needlessly due to inadequate appreciation of the importance of a well-developed system of 'Damage Control', as it came to be called. The Second World War saw a more intensified study of what became almost a science in itself, and classic instances such as HMS *Kelly* and HMCS *Nabob* proved that with well-trained Damage Control teams a ship that would formerly have been abandoned could be rendered sufficiently watertight to be sailed scores of miles to safety.

To avoid confusion and calamity it was part of the system that pipes running through the ship were painted a different colour according to their contents or use. DC exercises were naturally carried out frequently, and often combined with first aid drill. The contributor who communicated the previous song recalls that in the mid-1960s there was one chorus which 'achieved almost the status of a shanty amongst my first aid parties on HMS *Ghurka*, usually sung to hapless volunteer "casualties" as they were being hauled about upside-down in Neil-Robertson stretchers. Last line sung in 22-part harmony':

21 *Damage Control Song*
(Tune: 'Roses are Red, My Love')

Firemains are red, my love,
Fresh water's blue,
Salt water's green, my love,
But not as green as you.
AS GREEN AS YOOOOO.

All voyages, however perilous or uncomfortable, were bound to come to an end. If the vessel did not actually sink then the dockside or anchorage had to be reached, and that was the part the sailor loved best. But first he had to prepare for the long-awaited 'run ashore'. All 'dhoby sessions' were enjoyable to a degree, with the chance to switch off mentally and take advantage of the wash-room acoustics with a good sing-song while rubbing out your smalls, but the one on the eve of the first trip ashore was always especially joyous. Whatever the occasion, however, dhobying went better with a song, and if that song happened to be relevant to the occasion, so much the better:

22 *Onward Christian Soldiers*
(Tune: 'Onward Christian Soldiers')

Onward Christian sailors,
Scrub and wash your clothes.
Where the dirties come from
Lord Almighty knows.
I've got fourteen pieces
And one hammock to scrub,
But I cannot do it,
Someone's got the tub.

'Onward Christian sailors,
Scrub and wash your clothes'

39

Onward Christian sailors,
While there's life there's hope.
How the devil can I do my dhobying,
Someone's pinched my soap.

In the days of Port Divisions, when a rating was attached to one of three Naval Commands, Portsmouth, Plymouth or Chatham, for his entire career, the approach to that port after a long absence could be a sentimental, perhaps even a nostalgic progress. For many married men, wherever their origins, it had become home, with house, wife and children ashore and, whether married or not, those men at 'harbour stations' on the upper deck must often have felt a warm sense of anticipation as the well-known landmarks passed astern. Grubby cherubs in Portsmouth and Gosport may have learned few nursery rhymes from their sailor fathers, but they could lisp the matelot's guide for entering the harbour:

23 *Rhyme for Entering Portsmouth Harbour*

First the Nab,
Then the Warner,
Blockhouse Fort
And Shithouse Corner.

There was no tune to this that I can recall, it was simply chanted, but a correspondent tells me that the following variant was sung to the opening of 'Cwm Rhondda':

First the Nab,
And then the Warner,
Blockhouse Spit
And Submarine Corner.

The Nab: Nab Tower.
The Warner: The Warner Lightship.
Blockhouse Fort: The point on the Gosport side of Portsmouth Harbour

mouth. Part of HMS *Dolphin*, the submarine base.

Shithouse Corner: The sailor's nickname for North Corner, part of Portsmouth Dockyard. In the second version 'Submarine Corner' refers to the fact that, after passing Blockhouse Fort at the harbour mouth, a submarine, instead of proceeding up harbour, would make a sharp turn to port in order to reach its base.

Arrival in harbour meant, for some, a draft to barracks or direct to some other ship. It could be a time for regretful farewells, but not always:

24 *Take My Tip, Pack Your Grip*
(Tune: 'Bye Bye Blackbird')

> Take my tip, pack your grip,
> Get right off this bleeding ship,
> Bye bye *Loch Lomond*.
> Dump my gear upon the quay,
> Then no more you'll see of me,
> Bye bye *Loch Lomond*.
> I will leave the Jaunty far behind me,
> Where that lousy bastard cannot find me.
> So take my tip, pack your grip,
> Get right off this bleeding ship,
> *Loch Lomond*, bye bye.

The contributor points out that any ship's name could be substituted for *Loch Lomond*, so it seems that its use was not confined to that particular vessel.

The sight of other ships snugly tied up alongside or riding safely at anchor could produce feelings of resentment if it always seemed to be the same ones every time. This was particularly the case in time of war, when greater perils had to be faced by crews of sea-going vessels (see 'The Twenty-Third Flotilla Song', No. 69). The feeling was even more acute if the ships in question were those of our transatlantic allies:

25 *Damn Fine Kids in Harbour*
(Tune: 'The United States Marine)

From the Halls of Montezuma
To the shores of Tripoli
There's a buzz going round the harbour
That the Yanks are off to sea.
With a gallon of Coca Cola
And a bloody great tub of ice-cream,
Oh they're damn fine kids in harbour,
But oh my Christ at sea!

I have an incomplete second stanza, but if Americans were present when this song was struck up I doubt if it could ever get as far as a second stanza!

Although voiced in the first person, much the same sentiment probably lies behind the next piece, aimed at those ship's companies who, to their colleagues in overworked sea-going vessels at least, seemed always to be enjoying the relatively relaxing eight-to-five dockyard routine:

26 *The Dockyard Cavalry*
(Tune: 'Our Director', March by Bigelow)

We're a shower of bastards,
Bastards are we.
We are the Navy,
The Dockyard Cavalry.

We're a shower of bastards,
Bastards are we.
We'd rather fuck than fight,
We're the Dockyard Cavalry.

Besides those ships' companies refitting there were other groups of land-based personnel, those in shore establishments such as air stations, training camps and Royal Naval Barracks. There were three of the latter, one for each Port Division, and in theory most of the

42

manpower they contained was transient, comprising men awaiting draft to a sea-going ship. However, in the days before computerised central drafting, when the whole business was conducted on a human basis within each barracks, opportunities for graft and corruption at the Drafting Office were manifold and certainly had their existence in Jack's suspicious mind, if not in reality. While some were whisked off to sea perhaps within a week or two of arriving from a ship, certain other individuals, the human counterparts of those ships with everlasting refits, seemed to remain in barracks year in and year out, earning for themselves the nickname 'Barrack Stanchions'. It was the cherished dream of practically everyone that these favoured few would one day receive their come-uppance and be ousted from their snug berth, and without a doubt the best-known song on this subject, in fact the best-known song in the Royal Navy, is the one which follows.

Rather than give one of the numerous traditional variants (nearly every sailor knows a version) I have preferred instead simply to reproduce, for reference purposes, Mr John Bush's original words, written in Devonport Barracks in the 1920s. The second stanza has virtually died out, but I have received it in fragmentary form from one contributor. Mr Bush, who left the Navy under the 'Geddes Axe' and returned to the heart of the Midlands, had no idea, until I told him, that his modest piece had become a genuine folk song.

27 *I was Walking through the Dockyard in a Panic*
(Tune: 'I Wonder, Yes I Wonder')

I was walking through the Dockyard in a panic
When I met a matelot old and grey,
Upon his back he had his bag and hammock,
And this is what I heard him say:

Chorus
I wonder, yes I wonder,
Has the Jaunty made a blunder
When he served this draft-chit out for me?
For years I've been a stanchion,
I'm the pride of Jago's mansion,
It's a shame to send me off to sea.

I like my 'Pride of Keyham' and I like my week-end leave,
And I always bring the Western to the Chief
(GOOD MORNING CHIEF!)
Oh I wonder, yes I wonder,
Has the Jaunty made a blunder
When he served this draft-chit out for me?

Shall I wander out the sunny Straits in glory
On a trooper that is chock-a-block?
If I speak to shipmates who have gone before me
They are sure to double up with shock.

Chorus:
I wonder, yes I wonder,
Has the Jaunty made a blunder
When he served this draft-chit out for me?
For though we've lots of funnels
We're never rolling gunnels
And I'm always home in time for tea.
I've gazed upon the ocean while walking on the Hoe,
Though I own that that was very long ago
(SO LONG AGO!)
But t'ain't no use to holler,
I'll have to raise a dollar
And wangle back to RNB

NB: At least until the Second World War the customary lower-deck
pronunciation of 'leave' was 'leaf', though it is heard rarely nowadays. Thus,
in the middle of the first chorus, Mr Bush has used it as a rhyme for 'Chief'.

Mr Bush told me that the Chief Petty Officer who dealt with his
requests for week-end leave at Devonport Barracks in those days was a
fanatical Plymouth Argyle fan. These leave requests had to be
submitted first thing Monday morning, when the Chief's mood
would vary according to Argyle's result the previous Saturday. He it
was who determined whether or not a request for week-end leave
should go forward to the Divisional Officer, and even when it did his
recommendation one way or the other was seldom disregarded. It
soon became apparent that if Argyle had lost you stood precious little
chance of getting your leave, but if they had won then Chiefy, all
sunshine and bonhomie, would be unlikely to refuse anyone,
especially if the requestman was cunning enough to masquerade as a

44

fellow-supporter of Argyle. The trick was to approach him carrying a copy of the *Western Morning News*, containing a write-up of Argyle's successful match and, while handing over the request, make an enthusiastic but ostensibly spontaneous reference to the happy result. It hardly ever failed.

Looked at from a detached standpoint such a state of affairs is naturally a cause for amusement, but it carries a more sober connotation, inasmuch as it was upon the weather-cock caprices of such moody underlings that so many of the Royal Navy's more commonplace decisions were often permitted to rest, decisions which none the less could affect the liberties, welfare and general quality of life of those entrusted to their charge.

The 'barrack stanchion' in Mr Bush's song was clearly either a 'native', someone born and bred in the Plymouth area, or at least a married man resident in the port and consequently 'rationed ashore' (RA). Hence his reference to being 'always home in time for tea'. Yet there were many others who had no home and family nearby. These 'non-natives', especially when shortage of funds precluded 'big eats' ashore, were forced to take their meals in barracks:

28 Dining Hall Song
(Tune: 'Side by Side')

See the crowd in the evening
Outside the Dining Hall door,
I wonder what they're doing there
And what they're waiting for?
They're all waiting for something,
I wonder what it can be?
They've just had their dinner,
I presume they want their tea.

Chorus
For they ain't got a barrel of money,
There's nothing about it that's funny,
They can't go ashore
So they're outside the door,
Side by Side.

Burgoo for their breakfast,

45

Gash for dinner and tea,
And though they're very near starving
They're as happy as happy can be.
When they've all had their 'Jago's' and parted
They'll be the same as they started,
Hungry for bread,
Bloody near dead,
Side by side.

The contributor of this song had 'morning' instead of 'evening' in the first line, which seems illogical.

At sea there was no such thing as a dining hall, and lower-deck personnel ate where they lived and slept. While Chief and Petty Officers had the services of a messman the ordinary sailors had to fetch and carry for themselves. The next chorus refers to the person known as 'Cook of the Mess', a job undertaken daily by different ratings in turn, in addition to normal duties. No cooking was involved, their task being to prepare the food and carry it to the galley to be cooked. When the bugler sounded 'Cooks to the Galley' they brought the food back to their mess and served it to their messmates. After the meal they washed up. They were also responsible for drawing the mess rum ration.

29 *Cook of the Mess*

I'm cook of the mess,
I'm full of zest,
And for the lads I do my best,
Then up on deck I do the rest,
I'm having a busy day.

On small ships there was often only enough fresh food carried to last the first five days or so, after which it was up to the ingenuity of the cook. Some were imaginative, others were not. For the crew it was all very much a lottery:

46

'I'm cook of the mess,
I'm full of zest'

30 The Cook

Our cook is the king of the bully-beef Navy,
He's cooked it with soup, he's cooked it with gravy,
He's stewed it, he's grilled it, and he's bloody well fried it.
Bully-beef pies, bully-beef pasties, and he's bloody well boiled it.
He's cooked it standing, he's cooked it lying,
And if he had wings he'd cook it flying.
Bully-beef curries, bully-beef hash, bully-beef and chips,
Our bloody cook is the king of all HM ships.

New entries to the Royal Navy, and other juniors under training, could hardly expect preferential treatment where catering was concerned, and their first impression of Service food must have done little to ease their apprehension of the life that lay ahead. They were mostly fast-growing teenagers and, as every mother knows, no

47

amount of food could have satisfied them. Recourse to the canteen, if funds allowed, was the only solution. All the same, whatever the culinary shortcomings, things were surely never as bad as the boys of HMS *Ganges*, at Shotley, implied:

31 Shotley Stew
(Tune: 'A Little Bit of Heaven Fell')

There's half a pound of bully-beef left from the month before,
And half a yard of sausages found on the canteen floor,
One or two old ham-bones which were minus of the meat,
And two old tins of meat and veg. the dog refused to eat.
They took it to the galley and they let it boil all day,
They topped it up with Number Nines to pass the time away,
And when they finished boiling it, it tasted just like glue,
They gave it to the *Ganges* boys
And called it Shotley Stew.

Whether in a shore establishment or on a ship, when your pay was spent it was a case of staying on board and eating what the Navy gave you, but when pay-day came it was a different matter. With pubs and restaurants beckoning and money in your pocket there was no need to remain on board for the evening meal:

32 Well I Couldn't Care Less
(Tune: 'The Girl I Left Behind Me')

Well I couldn't care less for the killick of the mess
Or the Buffer of the working party.
I'm pushing off ashore at a quarter past four,
I'm Jack-me-bleedin'-hearty.

And even if you did not belong to the watch due for shore leave, with a lot of nerve and a little help from a courageous friend you could wangle your way past the gangway scrutineers. As the lads sang in the mid-1960s:

33 *Pretend You're Red Watch*
(Tune: 'Pretend')

Pretend you're red watch when you're blue,
It isn't very hard to do.
Your oppo's station card will do, my friend,
If only you'll pretend.

Not everyone accepted shore leave when it was available. This might be due to financial embarrassment, or perhaps the mind baulked at the bothersome business of bathing, shaving and shifting into Number Ones. As often as not the reason was simply downright weariness. Whatever the explanation, some there were who preferred to stretch out on the cushions with a book, write letters, or catch up with their dhobying. But if their company ashore was deemed indispensable by their messmates they were unlikely to be able to follow their inclination without harassment. Around 1968 sailors on HMS Barrossa employed a parody of a current pop song on such occasions:

34 *'Barrossa' Jack*
(Tune: 'Grocer Jack' or 'Theme from a Teenage Opera')

Barrossa Jack, *Barrossa* Jack,
Get off your back, go into town,
Don't let them down,
Your oppos.

Before going ashore it was necessary to get spruced up, not just to pass inspection by the Officer-of-the-Watch, but to impress the girls. Within the restrictions of his uniform the sailor was still able to assert a touch of individuality, and changing fashions did not pass him by completely:

35 *The Sailors of the Present Day*

Now the sailors of the present day, they are all right,
They smoke cigarettes and part their hair in front.
Instead of Bos'un's tallow Cherry Blossom's all the go,
And I question whether they could stow a bunt.
They wear watches on their lanyards now, m'boys, instead of knives,
And for their grinders they use special paste.
I wonder what would Nelson say if he were alive
And all our present Navy of a taste?
Someone ought to tell him of it, what say chums?
Such goings-on are shameful to behold.
Oh I'd like to be a swab and serve them out,
For I am a warrior bold.

The contributor of this song describes it as 'A ditty of 50 years ago, sung usually by a three-badged AB One, Tom Smith of Cheltenham, either on the *Chatham* or *Southampton*, East Indies Squadron.'

'Fifty years ago' would date the song around 1920, though it is almost certainly considerably older than that. No doubt the young sailors of Tom Smith's day must now, in their turn, be shaking their heads in disbelief to see their successors strolling ashore in their motley civilian gear, indistinguishable from their Merchant Navy cousins.

AT LIBERTY

36 The King's Horses, the King's Men
(Tune: 'King's Horses')

The King's horses, the King's men,
They've all gone ashore and they're bagging off again,
The King's horses and the King's men.
Some dressed in scarlet, some dressed in gold,
Some of the bastards are too bloody old,
The King's horses and the King's men.
There they go, on their toes.
Chasing queries I suppose,
Every time they get their pay
Slap another pusher in the family way.
Dirty shower o' bastards, damned if they ain't
About as handy as a matelot with a can of paint,
The King's horses and the King's men.

This parody of a popular song of the 1930s sets the scene of Jack's various adventures in this 'run-ashore' section. Not surprisingly, most songs in this category involve women in some way or other. One of the exceptions is the following ditty sung by trainee sailors at HMS *Raleigh*, the shore establishment at Torpoint, Cornwall, around 1959–60. These new recruits, many of them fresh from city backgrounds throughout Britain, looked on their initial posting to this comparatively bleak and remote corner of the realm as a form of banishment. Small wonder that with the advent of weekend or seasonal leave their first concern was not girls but the speediest way to get back to what they regarded as civilisation.

37 The 'Raleigh' Song
(Tune: 'What Shall We Do With a Drunken Sailor?')

What do we do when we leave *Raleigh*?
What do we do when we leave *Raleigh*?
What do we do when we leave *Raleigh*?
Early in the morning.

Run like hell for the nearest station (3)
Early in the morning.

What do we do when we get to the station? (3)
Early in the morning.

Catch a train to civilisation (3)
Early in the morning.

What do we do in civilisation? (3)
Early in the morning.

Run like hell for the nearest boozer (3)
Early in the morning.

What do we do when we get to the boozer? (3)
Early in the morning.

Drink to the health of the boys in *Raleigh* (3)
Early in the morning.

Hooray up she rises (3)
Early in the morning.

The longer a man served the weaker became this urge to rush 'up the line' at every opportunity (war service excepted of course). Time provided the experiences and familiarity which so often cause us to modify our initial aversion to certain people and places and, seasonal leaves apart, in home waters Jack tended more and more to seek his pleasures closer at hand, in the immediate vicinity of the host port, in much the same way as he did when abroad. And similar hazards awaited him:

38 *I Hopped up on the Gangway*
(Tune: See Appendix D)

I hopped up to the gangway and I hailed the picket boat,
I landed safe in Queen Street being just three years afloat,
With my bundle on my back and my pussers crabs so neat
I jammed my helm well over and I steered for Voller Street.

Chorus
Singing hi diddly hi hi ho
Hi diddly hi di ay
Hi hi de do day hey
Hi did e hi hi hey.

My Bradburys came unravelled and I lost the standing part,
Met with a fair young maiden and she fairly took my heart.
In the middle of the night in came her fancy bloke,
In the morning both eyes filled up likewise my leave I broke.

Got collared by the Water Rats and taken straight aboard,
Got before the Bloke and I couldn't say a word,
'Stop his pay, stop his leave, in addition to the Scale,
'Dip him one Good Conduct badge and send him off to jail.'

I picked up a yard and a quarter of flannel and some serge
Likewise some blue jeans, oh the Pusser opened his eyes,
'A sovereign for the lot, you can buy it if you please
'And lash your blinking scran chum up to sardines, jam and cheese.'

Now all my jolly shipmates this warning take from me,
Never pick up a pail of slops to raise a Pusser's fee,
If you do it's black-list and it ain't for you to brag
You'll find yourself in the old cell flat or else in the old scran bag.

Here we have a song of particular interest. While its jargon seems
mostly to belong to the twentieth century the style owes more to the
nineteenth. If the term 'Bradburys' occurred in the original version
the song cannot date from earlier than 1914 (see Glossary).

And, for all the penalties paid and painful lessons learned, half a
century later muzzy-headed Jack could still fall in for more than his
fair share of folly on the shore. He could still make up songs about it
too:

53

39 Scrumpy Wine
(Tune: 'Summer Wine')

I went ashore last night, my pockets did jingle jang,
Down to the Ideal pub, I went there with the gang.
Pissed up on scrumpy till just on closing time,
Then I spewed up again on scrumpy wine.
Oh, oh, scrumpy wine.

Woke up this morning and my eyes were full of grit.
I'd wet the bed again, and now I'm in the shit.
So take my ID card, for I'll confess my crime,
And never again will I drink that scrumpy wine.
Oh, oh, scrumpy wine.

Now the Jossman said to me, 'You stokers, you're all fools,
'And now you've been and broken the biggest of all rules.
'So grab your hat my friend, for you'll be doing time,
'You're on Commander's Report at half past nine.'
Oh, oh, scrumpy wine.

The Commander said to me, 'Now Stokes don't shoot no lines,
'You've been before me now forty-seven times.'
He then reassured me that I ought to stick to limes,
And then he lashed me up – fourteen days nines.
Oh, oh, scrumpy wine.

Across the harbour from Portsmouth, the scene of the two previous escapades, lies the borough of Gosport, its junior neighbour and the setting for another unique composition. In style and spirit it can rank alongside the best of the old sailing-ship ditties on the same subject. The author was clearly a cut above the usual standard of RN songwriters, yet he (or they) remains anonymous.

40 Gosport Nancy
(Tune: See Appendix D)

Gosport Nancy she's my fancy
She's the girl to make good sport.

How she'll greet you when she meets you
When your ship gets into port.
All the Gosport ladies they love a sailor man
But for finding a way to spend your pay
There's none like Gosport Nan.

Gosport ladies love their gargle
Gosport girls they goes their tot.
Rum and brandy, gin and shandy,
Gosport girls will drink the lot.
All the Gosport ladies they swigs the flowing can
But for knocking it back with Honest Jack
There's none like Gosport Nan.

Gosport girls they're good at dancing
They're the best there is no doubt
When the music sets them prancing
How they fling their skirts about.
All the Gosport ladies they do the French Can-Can
But for real high kicks and fancy tricks
There's none like Gosport Nan.

Gosport Nancy keeps a parlour
Where the boys can take their ease.
She will wake you, yes she'll shake you
She will do whatever you please.
All the Gosport ladies they do the best they can
But for making a bed for a sailor's head
There's none like Gosport Nan.

We are left to wonder whether Gosport Nancy was a real person or a figment of the writer's imagination, but no such doubt exists regarding the ladies in the next offering, a perfect example of Royal Navy fantasy-humour, with the sailor's fertile imagination running wild. Because it is found in such widely divergent forms, ranging from the messdeck-bawdy to the wardroom-respectable, with the euphemistic use of the word 'hat', I give three versions of the song, which is often known as 'Rig of the Day':

41 *Four Girls of Portsmouth Town*

There were four girls of Portsmouth Town
And they were drinking wine, sir.
The subject of their conversation
Was 'Hers is bigger than mine', sir.

Now the first one was an Admiral's wife
And she was dressed in blue, sir,
And in one corner of the funny little thing
There was a long-boat's crew, sir.
There was a long-boat's crew, my boys,
The rowlocks and the oars,
And in the other corner the Marines were forming fours.

Chorus
She had those dark and stormy eyes
And a whizzbang up her crumpet
She was one of those old-fashioned ladies,
One of the old brigade.

The next one was a fireman's wife
And she was dressed in red, sir,
And in one corner of the funny little thing
There was a horse's head, sir.
There was a horse's head, my boys,
The bridle and the bit,
And in the other corner was a bloody great heap of shit.

The next one was a fisherman's wife
And she was dressed in green, sir,
And in one corner of the funny little thing
There was a soup tureen, sir.
There was a soup tureen, my boys,
The ladle and the soup,
And in the other corner the Air Force looped the loop.

My informant was unable to recall the fourth verse.

42 Sailors' Wives
(Tune: See Appendix D)

The first one was the stoker's wife
And she was dressed in brown,
And in one corner of her hat there was a bunker upside-down,
A bunker upside down, my boys, the shovels and the rakes
And in the other corner was a bunch of boiler plates.

Chorus
And she'd a dark and roving eye
And her hair hung down to her ankles
She was one of the best girls
Out of Pompey Town.

The next one was the gunner's wife
And she was dressed in green,
And in one corner of her hat she stowed the magazine,
She stowed the magazine, my boys, the powder and the shells,
And in the other corner was a nine-point-four as well.

The next one was the bunting's wife
And she was dressed in black,
And in one corner of her hat she stowed the Union Jack,
She stowed the Union Jack, my boys, and ensigns by the score,
And in the other corner was the starboard semaphore.

The next one was the bo'sun's wife
And she was dressed in red,
And in one corner of her hat she stowed the deep-sea lead,
She stowed the deep-sea lead, my boys, a loose-lead line as well,
And in the other corner was a matelot doing cells.

The next one was the cox'n's wife
And she was dressed in blue,
And in one corner of her hat she stowed the cutter's crew.
She stowed the cutter's crew, my boys, the rowlocks and the oars,
And in the other corner battalions forming fours.

43 *The Captain's Ball*

And then there came the Snotty's wife
And she was dressed in grey,
And in one corner of her hat she carried his bob a day.
She carried his bob a day, my lads, the patches and the dirk,
And in the other corner his great dislike of work.

And then there came the Pusser's wife
And she was dressed in pink,
And in one corner of her hat she carried the off-ice ink.
She carried the off-ice ink, my lads, the pencils and the nibs,
And in the other corner a ruddy great box of dibs.

And then there came the Pilot's wife
And she was dressed in red,
And in one corner of her hat she carried the deep-sea lead.
She carried the deep-sea lead, my lads, the sextant and the log,
And in the other corner his great dislike of fog.

And then there came the C'mmander's wife
And she was dressed in mauve,

'And then there came the C'mmander's wife'

And in one corner of her hat she carried the wardroom stove.
She carried the wardroom stove, my lads, the brightwork and the
paint,
And in the other corner language to shock a saint.

And then there came the Gunner's wife
And she was dressed in green,
And in one corner of her hat she carried the magazine.
She carried the magazine, my lads, the cordite and the shell,
And in the other corner a six-inch gun as well.

And then there came the Watchkeeper's wife
And she was dressed in white,
And in one corner of her hat she carried the masthead light.
She carried the masthead light, my lads, the red and green ones too,
And in the other corner the whole of the sea-boat's crew.

And then there came the Bo'sun's wife
And she wasn't dressed at all,
And in one corner of her hat she carried the Bo'sun's call.
She carried the Bo'sun's call, my lads, the spunyarn and the rope,
And in the other corner a ruddy great box of soap.

And then there came the Jimmy's wife
And she was dressed in brown,
And in one corner of her hat she carried his half-a-crown.
She carried his half-a-crown, my lads, the messdeck and the cooks,
And in the other corner were the fo'c'sle and the hooks.

And then there came the Messman's wife
And she was dressed in silk,
And in one corner of her hat she carried the con-densed milk.
She carried the con-densed milk, my lads, the sugar and the tea,
And in the other corner was the muck he served at sea.

And then there came the Chiefy's wife
And she was dressed in gold,
And in one corner of her hat she carried the fore stokehold.
She carried the fore stokehold, my lads, the engine-room as well,
And in the other corner was a bearing hot as hell.

And then there came the Bandy's wife
And she was dressed in fawn,

And in one corner of her hat she carried the tenor horn.
She carried the tenor horn, my lads, and the eu-phon-i-um,
And in the other corner was a damn great big bass drum.

And then there came the PTI's wife
And she was dressed in cream,
And in one corner of her hat she carried the football team.
She carried the football team, my lads, the forwards and the backs,
And in the other corner all the little jumping jacks.

And then there came the Doctor's wife
And she was dressed in drill,
And in one corner of her hat she carried a stomach pill.
She carried a stomach pill, my lads, as large as any seen,
And in the other corner a copy of the boat routine.

And then there came the Torp.'s wife
And she was dressed in black,
And in one corner of her hat she carried a torpedo track.
She carried a torpedo track, my lads, curving round and round,
And in the other corner was an earth that he had found.

And then there came old Stripey's wife
And she was dressed in wool,
And in one corner of her hat she carried a tankard full.
She carried a tankard full, my lads, of frothy foaming ale,
And in the other corner the Patrol being told the tale.

And then there came the Soldier's wife
And she was dressed in checks,
And in one corner of her hat she carried the leathernecks.
She carried the leathernecks, my lads, and all their hob-nailed boots,
And in the other corner a drummer was sounding salutes.

And then there came the Captain's wife
And she was dressed so sleek,
And in one corner of her hat she carried a load of teak.
She carried a load of teak, my lads, a mighty heavy load,
And in the other corner a house up Vernon Road.

There was nothing fanciful and very little for the sailor to laugh at
in the fact that until the toll-gate on Stonehouse Bridge at the

western end of Plymouth's Union Street was dispensed with in the 1920s the Army was excused toll while the matelot had to pay the full amount of one halfpenny, despite the bridge being by far the most convenient and direct route from the city back to Devonport Dockyard. The 'Ha'penny Gate', as it was called, belonged to the estate of the Earl of Mount Edgcumbe, a fact which gave rise to the following supplication:

44 *Lordy Edgcumbe Good and Great*
(Tune: 'Twinkle, Twinkle, Little Star')

Lordy Edgcumbe, good and great,
Open wide the Ha'penny Gate,
While the soldiers go through free
Sailors pay an 'a'penny.

Lord Mount Edgcumbe, lord divine,
All the hakey fish are thine,
All the fishes in the sea,
Lord Mount Edgcumbe, belong to thee.

The last two lines of the first verse varied. Another form was:

Let the sailors go through free,
Make the soldiers pay one pen-nee.

A correspondent writing in the *Western Evening Herald* in 1965 states:

It was always a sore point with the Navy that it had to pay and the military did not. There was many a tussle, late at night, when the Jolly Jacks would try to rush the gate, and the gatemen would snatch their caps, for future identification I suppose.

I first heard the opening lines of the song from my late father back in Gosport, long before I set foot in Plymouth, but, if an old shipmate of his is correct, in his seagoing days Dad also used to warble his own personal adaptation:

Lordy Edgcumbe, good and great,
Send me down the first-class rate.

With the removal of the 'Ha'penny Gate' it was only natural that the 'Lordy Edgcumbe' jingle should fall into disuse and eventually disappear from the sailor's repertoire. Such is far from the case with another indigenous Plymouth song, one which was the 'signature tune' or 'anthem' of the Devonport Port Division for generations and is still sung. For his theme Jack looked westward to the land of the Cornish pasty or 'Tiddy-Oggie', usually shortened to 'Oggie', and this seems as good a place as any to correct a misconception which seems to be gaining ground more and more as the years go by, to the effect that the 'war-cry' 'OGGIE! OGGIE! OGGIE!' is the property of the Welsh. How this fallacious notion developed is a puzzle. I suspect after-match rugby get-togethers were initially responsible for the transmigration, the delusion later being lent authority by the comedian Max Boyce, so that now even Welsh politicians have been sufficiently gulled to conclude the occasional speech with what they deem to be a patriotic exhortation.

The truth of the matter is that by rights the cry is the exclusive trademark of 'Guzz' Royal Navy personnel, and although it has become detached for the purpose of supporting sports teams and field-gun crews it correctly belongs at the end of 'The Oggie Song', where it is followed by the response: 'OINK! OINK! OINK!' One only has to hear Welshmen erroneously shouting 'OY! OY! OY!' for proof that their claim to the chant is quite spurious.

In his book *I Joined the Navy and Saw the World* Ivor Burston describes how, at the Royal Naval Barracks, Devonport, in 1943, he helped write the original lyrics, and adds: 'This was first sung in the Beer Bar and Batchy Payne was the pianist.'

45 *The Oggie Song*

Where be going to Jagger?
I be going to Looe.
Gor! Bugger Jagger!
I be going there too.

Chorus
Oh 'ow' 'appy us will be
When us gets to the Westcountree
Where the oggies grow on trees
Gor! Bugger Jagger!

Up the Camborne Hill we go
Down to Helston Ferry
Come on Jagger, don't be late,
Come on Jagger, hurry.

Chorus Oh 'ow 'appy, etc.

Half a pound of flour and marge
Makes lovely clacker
Just enough for you and me
Gor! Bugger Jagger!

Chorus: Oh 'ow 'appy, etc.

You make fast, I'll make fast,
Make fast the dinghy,
You make fast, I'll make fast, (or 'kiss my arse')
Make fast the dinghy,
And we'll all go back to Oggie Land,
To Oggie Land, to Oggie Land,
Yes we'll all go back to Oggie Land,
Where they don't know sugar from
Tissue paper, tissue paper, marmalade and jam.

Shout: OGGIE! OGGIE! OGGIE!

Response: OINK! OINK! OINK!

Supplementary chorus:
On the quarter deck I lie
Have some starry-gazy pie
Have another pint of beer with I
Gor! Bugger Jagger!

To indicate the tune(s) to which the above words are sung is a little complicated. The first three verses and chorus are based on the hymn 'There is a Happy Land, Far, Far Away'. The remainder of the song is to the tune 'Marching to Pretoria', apart from the final two lines, which have a tune of their own. The 'Make fast the dinghy' quatrain was taken over, I believe, from a marching song of the Corps of Royal Engineers. In a TV play called 'Stocker's Copper' the song was heard being sung, somewhat surprisingly, to the tune 'Pop Goes the Weasel'. I have never heard it sung to that tune, and I would hazard a guess that the producers were provided with the words only and were misled by the line 'Half a pound of flour and marge.'

No significance should be attached to the fact that the foregoing Portsmouth songs all involve the fair sex whereas in the three items from the Plymouth area the girls do not even rate a mention. Rest assured that wherever they were from and wherever they went, sailors would usually be sailors. Nevertheless, in any port, at home or abroad, the lasses were entitled to their preferences:

46 *Chinese Maiden's Lament*
(Tune: 'What a Friend we Have in Jesus')

Me no likee English sailor
When Yankee sailor come ashore.
English sailor plenty money
Yankee sailor plenty more.
Yankee sailor call me ducky darling
English sailor call me Chinese whore.
Yankee sailor only shag for short time
English sailor shag for evermore.

'Join the Navy and see the world' was a common enough axiom, but where a prolonged spell on one station was involved the novelty could wear off, and not every matelot viewed the mysterious East as an exotic paradise:

47 *Roll on the Boat that Takes Me Home*

I went ashore in Singapore
And there I broke my leave.
When I came on board the Jaunty
Had something up his sleeve.
He said, 'You're due for a forty-two
'And a mansion up the hill,
'Go pack your kit.'
'Don't make us shit.'
But I packed it against my will.

Chorus
Roll on the boat, the boat that takes me home,
Free from this land of pox and fever.
Mosquitoes, bugs and flies
Get in my bloody eyes.
Roll on the boat that takes me home.

'Fleas' sometimes substituted for 'pox'.

Even Malta, with a far less oppressive climate than Singapore, was known to the sailor as the island of 'smells, yells and bells' back in the earlier years of this century, when the description was probably more apt than it is today. This chorus was popular in the 1930s.

48 *'Baa!' Go the Goats*
(Tune: See Appendix D)

'Baa!' go the goats
'Ow!' go the di-so-men
'Dong!' go the bells in the steeple
'Bang!' go the guns of destroyers doing night attacks
The hooter at St Angelo goes 'Peep! Peep! Peep!'

Inglis Gundry explains:

 (i) At the time milk was delivered direct from the goats.
 (ii) 'Ow!' was Maltese for 'Hello!' or 'Hi!', the boatman soliciting a fare.
(iii) The hooter on Fort St Angelo announced the landing of seaplanes.

Malta is also the scene for what must surely be one of the two classics of RN imaginative humour (the other being 'Jenny Wren Bride', No. 56). Taking for his model the serious American murder-ballad 'Frankie and Johnny' (itself modelled on an older English folk song), in which a jealous woman murders her man after catching him with a rival and ends up in the electric chair, the British sailor has a veteran lower-deck rating ('Stripey') two-timing his girl not with another woman but with a junior sailor ('OD'). In other words, unlike Johnny, Stripey is bisexual. Moreover, his murder is not carried out with a humdrum 'forty-four' but with the largest weapon in a battleship's armament. However, it is in dealing with Blondie's ultimate punishment that Jack produces his master-stroke of creative fancy, one that is firmly in the mainstream of the folk tradition.

49 *Stripey and Blondie*
(Tune: 'Frankie and Johnny')

Now come here and I'll tell you a story
It's all about Malta you know.
It's all about a Valletta-bound Jane
And a guy named Stripey Joe.

Chorus
He was her man, but he was doing her wrong.

Now Blondie was still in her twenties,
Stripey was past thirty-two.
Stripey was running Blondie
And an OD winger too.

Now Blondie she went round to Sliema,
Stripey hadn't been with the car,
And you all know the place that Blondie went,
It was a dive called the Cairo Bar.

Blondie walked into the Cairo,
Ordered a nice juicy Blue,
And over in the corner sat Stripey
And his OD winger too.

Stripey saw Blondie approaching,
He said, 'A sherry for Blondie please.'
'I don't want your sherry,' said Blondie,
'And get your hands off that OD's knees.'

The OD he blushed crimson,
The Cairo Bar it was packed,
And every matelot started whispering:
'I bet that OD's just been cracked.'

Blondie got into a di-so,
She rowed round to Bighi Bay,
She went aboard the *Warspite*
And took her fifteen-inch away.

Blondie rowed back round to Sliema,
Fifteen-inch as well,
And aiming by director
She blew the Cairo Bar to hell.

Now Blondie she's up in Corradino,
That's if she's still alive.
She's chamfering down that fifteen-inch
To make the barrel of a four-point-five.

Now this is the moral to the story
As any matelot can tell,
Never run an OD winger
And a blonde barmaid as well.

An alternative final verse runs:

Now this story has no moral,
It only goes to show what I've said,
That there's more than one Valletta-bound Jane
And they ain't in the blinking Med.

Blue: A brand of Maltese beer.
Corradino: The naval prison in Malta.

At the western end of the Mediterranean stands Gibraltar, a
British naval base since 1704. Small in area, yet not too densely
populated like Hong Kong, it was never noted among bluejackets as
an amatory hunting-ground, a fact which makes the following piece
of delicate indelicacy especially ironic:

50 *On Gibraltar's Slopes*
(Tune: 'The Red Flag')

On Gibraltar's slopes so firm and steep
A lovely maid lay down to sleep
And as she lay in sweet repose

A gust of wind blew up her clothes.
A three-badge matelot passing by
Turned to look with eager eye,
But as he gazed, to his despair,
He saw the red flag flying there.

Although geographically the final piece in this section is correctly placed between Gibraltar and home waters, it is open to question whether or not it strictly belongs under the heading 'At liberty', the sailor's presence on shore hardly being voluntary. Few shipwrecked mariners, however, could have had the kind of reception accorded the hero of this favourite piece of canteen whimsy, the substance of which could be said to put a fresh construction on the term 'At liberty'.

51 *I was Only Seventeen*
(Tune: 'Let the Rest of the World Go By')

I was only seventeen
When first I went to sea,
I was shipwrecked off the coast of France,
And just by chance
A woman in a boat
Grabbed me by the coat
And pulled me on the shore to dry.
Then much to my distress
She started to undress,
A map of Bonny Scotland tattooed upon her chest,
And further down,
To my surprise,
I saw the spot where Nelson lost his eye.
There was a map of the Portuguese
Tattooed upon her knees,
Japan and Singapore upon her thigh.
I was looking for Hong Kong
When her old man came along,
So I let the rest of the world go by.

DOCKYARD

Latest story from Devonport Dockyard: A dockyard worker was seen to crush two snails with his foot. When asked why he did it, he replied: 'I'm fed up with them. They've been following me around all day.'

Western Evening Herald, 12 September 1972

I greatly like the 'Dockyard Maties' (songs). I've had much experience of them (the maties) from both ships refitting and as a Dockyard officer as ACD Chatham and Master Attendant, Bermuda. The riggers are all right, being mostly naval pensioners, but the rest are (or were) just like what the ditties mock!

Commander R.D.P. Hutchinson RN (Retd)

Dockyard employees, past and present, would most likely regard the above quotes as a somewhat jaundiced view of their vocation but, as Commander Hutchinson suggests, they reflect a generally held, if tongue-in-cheek, opinion among sea-going personnel. One of the earliest songs I can remember from my Gosport boyhood, sung regularly around the house by my father and at times of celebration by the whole Tawney clan *en masse*, gives cynical expression to this sentiment:

52 Dockyard Mateys' Sons
(Tune: Based on 'Just Like the Ivy on the Old Garden Wall')

We are dockyard mateys' sons
Sitting on the dockyard wall,

Watching our poor fathers
Doing bugger all.
When we grow older
We'll be dockyard mateys too,
Just like our fathers,
With bugger all to do.

A less well-known jingle suggests that the dockyard worker is merely conserving his energy for the more important occasions, such as knocking-off time:

53 *Can a Dockyard Matey Run?*
(Tune: 'Come Ye Thankful People, Come')

Can a dockyard matey run?
Yes, by Christ, I've seen it done.
When the policeman rings the bell
He drops his tools and nips like hell,
Over planks and by the dock,
Exerting every ounce of strength he's got.
Can a dockyard matey run?
Yes, by Christ, I've seen it done.

In time of war, however, or at other moments of crisis such as the Falklands emergency, the dockyard labour force can be sufficiently galvanised to meet any challenge, and ships' refits, in the days of these songs at least, were usually on schedule. Taken all round, the naval man's persistent disparagement of the dockyard worker's capacity for industrious effort is more in the nature of good-humoured raillery inspired by frequent observation of his civilian counterpart's languid, shuffling progress from one point to another. At least one song, though, sung soon after HMS *Hood* was first commissioned in 1920, throws a small shaft of light upon the other side of the coin:

54 The Commissioning of HMS 'Hood'

You ought to go to Rosyth
And see them dock the *Hood*,
Dockyard maties running round
With bloody great lumps of wood.
The commander's on the fo'c'sle,
Skipper on the bridge,
Jimmy the One on the quarterdeck
Playing at ha'penny bridge.
Rajah, Rajah of the UJC.

We had a rotten Jaunty
Who never saw a gun.
He got a bleeding medal
For sharking sailor's rum.
Now the war is over
You should see that Jaunty run.
Rajah, Rajah of the UJC.

Another aspect of dockyard life is touched upon in the next item, a recitation rather than a song. In industry a variety of names (e.g. 'foreigners') are given to those artefacts, materials or provisions pilfered from one's employers. In the Admiralty service they are termed 'rabbits', and the practice is known as 'rabbitting'. Probably on account of more regular opportunities, dockyard employees are more prone to engage in rabbitting than uniformed personnel, though it must be said that the civilians risk harsher penalties. Some individuals indulge wholesale in the habit, and of them it often used to be said: 'If the Barracks bugler sounded off "Return Stores" his bleedin' house would fall down.'

This embittered rhyme is not a dockyard piece pure and simple, any more than was the preceding one, and it could have been included under 'At liberty', but it does serve to show that the odd sailor can have a more serious aversion to dockyard workers than do his fellows. Note that they are referred to as 'Dockyard Mateys', indicating that the speaker does not belong to Devonport Division but is a Portsmouth or Chatham rating committed to an enforced sojourn in 'Oggie-land' (a Devonport rating would have called them

71

'Dockyardees'). For all its blinkered venom 'Ode to Guzz' remains a remarkably potent piece of versification.

55 *Ode to Guzz*

Houses furnished with pusser's stores,
The Hoe, littered with Plymouth 'hoers',
Union street and all its bums,
Drake and his silly bastard drums,
Evil-speaking stingy Janners,
They ain't got no bleeding manners,
Dockyard mateys, loafing bastards,
Scrounging ticklers off their masters,
This lot just about sums up Guzz,
Roll on, roll on my bleeding doz.

The supreme composition concerning rabbitting is undoubtedly 'Jenny Wren Bride', or to give it its earlier title 'Pusser-built Bride'. It is difficult to estimate its date of origin, but if the verse mentioning HMS *Hood* was in the original version it must have been made up after 1920 (the requirements of rhyme preclude any other ship's name being used at that point). Once again Jack's predilection for bizarre imagery is given full rein.

56 *Jenny Wren Bride*
(Tune: 'My Bonny Lies Over the Ocean')

I've just come away from the wedding,
Oh lord I could laugh till I cried.
I'll never forget the relations I met
When I married my Jenny Wren bride.

Chorus
Married, married, I married my Jenny Wren bri-i-ide,
Married, married, I married my Jenny Wren bride.

Her father he works in the dockyard,
Her brother he owns a Marine Store,

And as for their habits, well talk about rabbits,
They've got half the dockyard ashore.

I asked her old man for a dowry,
He gave me a can of soft soap,
A bundle of waste and some polishing paste
And fifty-six fathoms of rope.

The present we got from her brother
Was twenty-four yards of blue jean,
Her cousin, the Crusher, he sent us note-paper,
Six packets of Service Latrine.

Her family hung flags in the churchyard
And they painted the hallway with flatting,
When out stepped the bride they all piped the side,
And she tripped on the coconut matting.

Her wedding-dress, lashed up with spunyarn,
Was made from an old whaler's sail.
On top of her head a dishcloth was spread,
With a spudnet in front for a veil.

Her petticoat was made out of hessian,
Her knickers were made of green baize,
While for her suspenders she'd a motor-boat's fenders
And two pusser's gaiters for stays.

Now most of the church congregation
Was made up of Wrens on the dole,
While in the back pew sat the six-inch gun's crew
And half of the standing patrol.

The parson got up in the pulpit.
He said, 'Who gives this woman away?'
Then a bloke from the *Hood* whispered: 'Blimey, I could,
'But let every dog have its day.'

Well now, I'm just off on me honeymoon,
I don't know what happens tonight,
But I've spoke to a few who declare that they do,
And they swear she's a bit of all right.

Our final dockyard song, a widely-popular one with generations of matelots, combines the bluejacket's prolific imagination with his often outrageous sense of irreverence. Given the pious decorum of today's men of the cloth the song is undeniably surrealistic, but had it been written at the time of the Restoration Navy it could have had a truer ring. Many of Pepys's naval chaplains carried their eccentricity to extremes:

> The Rev. George Bradford, for instance, who, after drinking six pints of beer, threw the seventh at the coxswain's head, took off his clothes, and swearing 'God damn (me), (I'm) a man-o-war', leapt over a wall, tore his shirt from his back, running up and down swearing as if he was a madman.
> (Cited by Christopher Lloyd in *The Nation and the Navy*, Cresset Press, 1961)

The opening words of the song are based on a solemn Victorian tear-jerker, 'The Volunteer Organist', which begins:

> The preacher in the village church one Sunday morning said,
> 'Our organist is ill today, will someone play instead?'

For his tune, however, the sailor has uncharacteristically turned to the English folk tradition. Variations of the text are numerous.

57 *The Preacher in the Dockyard Church*
(Tune: 'To Be a Farmer's Boy')

The preacher in the dockyard church
One Sunday morning said:
'Some dirty bastard's shit himself,
'I'll punch his bleeding head.'
Then up jumped Jack from the third row back,
And he spat a slimy gob,
'I am the one who shit himself,
'You can chew my carrotty kno-o-ob,
'You can chew my carrotty knob.'

A Jenny Wren walked down the aisle,
There was a fearful hush.
The preacher from the pulpit said:

74

'I think you're bleeding lush.'
A matelot staggered down the aisle
With the organ on his back.
The preacher from the pulpit said:
'You can waltz that bastard ba-a-ck,
'You can waltz that bastard back.'

WAR

While many of the songs from the two World War periods can be considered as expressing a 'worm's-eye' opinion about the lot of the rank-and-file individual in a global conflict, there are a few which attempt a straightforward record of some major event that took place in the centre of the world arena. Of these latter, some may be fairly reliable first-hand accounts while others owe more to the exaggerations and inaccuracies of third-hand gossip, and in this respect they tend to mirror both the strength and the weakness of corresponding songs from the days of sail.

The least satisfactory feature of this particular body of song, however, must be the sense of frustration induced by the realisation that so much pertaining to the 1914-18 war has been lost. Had a search been made considerably earlier among the host of participants still surviving at the time, this present section, I am sure, would not be so lop-sided in favour of the Second World War. As it is, we can only be thankful that the few songs following have been rescued.

58 Dardanelles Patrol Song
(Tune: 'Roaming in the Gloaming')

Rolling and patrolling
Outside the Dardanelles,
Waiting for the *Goeben*
So that we can test our shells.
We went up to Chanak
But we very soon came back,
Ain't it lovely rolling and patrolling?

At the outbreak of hostilities in 1914 the German cruiser *Goeben*, completed in 1912 and named after a general of the Franco-Prussian war, successfully eluded a British naval force in the Mediterranean to reach Constantinople and persuade Turkey to ally itself with Germany and Austria-Hungary, with the result that the Dardanelles passage was closed to the Allies for the remainder of the war. But the astonishing sequel to our modest little chorus is that, apart from a brief and rather disastrous sortie into the Aegean in January 1918, not only did the *Goeben* never re-emerge into the Mediterranean as was hoped, but, having been transferred to Turkey and renamed *Yavuz*, was still holed up in the Sea of Marmara 58 years later (*Sunday Telegraph*, 3 September 1972).

Not long after this, on 31 October 1914, the Royal Navy suffered its first defeat for over a century when a German force under Admiral Von Spee sank the *Good Hope* and *Monmouth* in a few minutes at the Battle of Coronel, off the Chilean coast. Admiral Sturdee was promptly despatched with the battle-cruisers *Inflexible* and *Invincible* to the Falkland Islands, where he caught up with the German force of two cruisers and three light cruisers on 8 December, sinking all but the light cruiser *Dresden*, which escaped, only to be caught and sunk off Juan Fernandez Isle three months later.

59 *Battle of the Falkland Islands*
(Tune: Based on 'Little Redwing')

One day at Port Stanley
The look-out man did see
Some smoke upon the horizon
'I wonder if that's Graf Von Spee?'
He sent the message quick
To the *Invincible* our flagship.
The admiral said, 'I'm shaving now
'But just you wait a while,
'I've got a score to settle for
'*Good Hope* and *Monmouth* of Coronel.'

Chorus
Oh Graf Von Spee your days are numbered
So pack your bag and make your will,

For you will find that you have blundered
Obeying orders from Kaiser Bill.

One ship involved in all three encounters was HMS *Glasgow*, and the
above is a rather garbled traditional fragment of a longer song (six
stanzas plus six differing 'choruses') which was 'composed and sung
by Messrs A.G. Wilson and C. Shrives' of *Glasgow*'s ship's company
and printed as a broadsheet under the title 'Revenge'. The fact that
part of their composition has survived orally suggests that *Glasgow*'s
crew took the song to their hearts, but it was probably the final
'chorus' that they sang with the deepest feeling:

And that's the tale of the Falkland battle
And tho' it's earned us an honoured name
It hasn't earned our return to England,
They recalled our squadron, but we remain.

A second song concerning the same action is still remembered by
Falkland Islanders:

60 *The Noble Eighth of December*
(Tune: See Appendix D)

When our fleet left Abrolhos rocks
To sweep the mighty ocean
That us could give the Germans socks
We had a mighty notion.
The *Invincible* and the *Inflexible*,
A noteworthy addition,
Would quickly sweep the German decks
And send them to perdition.

Chorus
Oh the glorious feat of the phantom fleet
We always will remember,
When we cleared the seas of Graf Von Spee
On the noble eighth of December.

Bold Sturdee took complete command
All on board his battle cruiser.

He knew the game was in his hands
And didn't mean to lose her.
The *Bristol, Glasgow, Cornwall, Kent,*
All keen to do their section,
So with *Carnarvon* off they went
In a southerly direction.

For ten long days we ploughed the main,
Our vigilance was tireless.
No news of us the foes could gain,
We did not use our wireless.
Port Stanley in the Falkland Isles
Was our first destination,
Another good three thousand miles
In the service of the nation.

We dropped the hook on Monday morn,
Coaled ship with speed terrific,
Expecting next to round the Horn
And sweep up the Pacific.
The cruisers *Monmouth* and *Good Hope*
Had there met with disaster.
We'd give the Kaiser no more rope
But show him who was master.

Next day the look-out on Sapper's Hill
Some foreign warships sighted.
The news went through us with a thrill
And all hands were delighted.
The *Dresden*, *Leipzig* and *Nürnberg*
Could all be seen with ease now,
Along with two armed merchantmen
And the *Scharnhorst* and the *Gneisenau*.

Each man was quickly at his post
And outside our ships soon steaming
Prepared to meet our foreign host
With ensigns gaily streaming.
But Graf Von Spee he stood aghast,
To fight as he regretted,
For two big ships with tripod masts
Was not what he expected.

The flagship sank the *Scharnhorst*,
The *Inflexible*, the *Gneisenau*,
And *Nürnberg*, who fought the *Kent*,
Lies underneath the seas now.
The *Leipzig* was the *Glasgow*'s bag,
Of her pluck you have no notion.
They sent her down to join her flag
At the bottom of the ocean.

Abrolhos rocks: Abrolhos Archipelago, about halfway between Salvador and Rio de Janeiro, Brazil.
From the rhymes in verses 5 and 7 it will be seen that in this traditional song *Gneisenau* is pronounced 'Neez-now'. (The contributor actually sang 'Geez-now'.)

Back in home waters the Harwich Naval Force, commanded throughout the 1914–18 war by Commodore (later Admiral Sir) Reginald Tyrwhitt, performed valuable service in the North Sea, beginning with its participation in the successful action off the Heligoland Bight on 28 August 1914 and including, from 1916 onwards, the protection of the weekly convoys that ran between the Shipwash Light-vessel off Orfordness and the Maas Lightship off the mouth of the river leading to Rotterdam, carrying such commodities as butter, cheese and eggs from the dairies of Holland, partly because Britain needed them and partly to make sure they were denied to Germany, which Britain was blockading. Though no meat was involved to the best of my knowledge, these escort duties were known as 'Beef Trips' (a slang term used by junior midshipmen in a different context), and by all accounts they were no picnic:

The escorting of the Dutch 'Beef Trip' during the
war was an unpleasant job when the weather was really
bad or foggy. Frankly we detested it . . . . Mines
were always our bugbear, for the submarines from
Zeebrugge were very busy. Indeed, the whole area between
Orfordness and the North Foreland soon became an ocean
graveyard. Our chart became dotted with little red-ink
symbols denoting sunken ships. At the end of 1916 it showed
no less than forty-three. The signals we so frequently received –
'The port of Harwich is closed due to mines' – rarely

seemed to make much difference. We went to sea just the same.
(Capt. Taprell Dorling, DSO, RN, 'Taffrail', in *Endless Story*,
Hodder & Stoughton, 1931)

I was in the Harwich Force. Was for hostilities only but finished
up serving nearly 30 years in the RN. My most vivid memories of
those days are not so much the endless days at sea, with decks
awash, doing 'Beef Trips' across the North Sea, but of the nights
spent in the canteen when boiler-cleaning at Parkestone Quay, and
the old song always sung was [as given below]. The *Dido* was the
Depot and Repair and Accommodation ship for destroyers at
Harwich in the First World War, pretty firmly secured to
Parkestone Quay for the purpose.

(Mr L. B. Horton)

61 *Harwich Naval Force Song*

Don't send away the *Dido*,
Don't send her out to sea.
If you send away the *Dido*
Then down comes Parkestone Quay.

The seafarer's dread of mines was understandable. A torpedo might
at least be detected by its track on occasions, but there was
something extra sinister about these silent, unseen 'eggs' lying in
wait to plant their explosive kiss of death upon a ship's hull. A
simple song, however, might help to soothe anxiety, and at the same
time as the canteen in Harwich rang to the *Dido* chorus, this is what
could be heard 450 miles to the north, in the canteen at Invergordon:

62 *Never Mind*
(Tune: 'If Your Face Should Lose Its Smile, Never Mind')

If the *Antrim* strikes a mine, never mind,
If we're always left behind, never mind.
The skipper's name is Lunn,
He's as cracked as old Ben Gunn,
If the *Antrim* strikes a mine, never mind.

For the record, *Antrim* survived the war and there is no record of anyone named Lunn commanding her during that time, but with no other versions to go by we have no way of knowing whether this piece originated with the crew of *Antrim* or some other ship with a two-syllable name.

On the other hand it is reasonable to suppose that the entire Senior Service, regardless of ship, must have echoed our final 1914–18 contribution throughout the whole war:

63 *We're Looking for the Kaiser*
(Tune: 'The Church's One Foundation')

We're looking for the Kaiser,
He does not come our way.
We've searched the mighty ocean
Right down to Chesapeake Bay,
And when we get to Berlin
The Kaiser he will say:
'Hock! Hock! Mein Gott! What a bloody fine lot
'Is the Navy of today.'

Whereas in August 1914 the Royal Navy had had the fillip of an immediate success at the Heligoland Bight, and even the Coronel defeat was emphatically avenged before the year was out, the Second World War began disastrously. On 17 September 1939 the aircraft-carrier HMS *Courageous* was sunk off the south-west of Ireland by *U-29* with the loss of 518 lives, and on 14 October 833 more men (and boys) were lost when *U-47* penetrated the defences of Scapa Flow to sink HMS *Royal Oak*. Britain had to wait until December, in fact, before any heartening news came from the Admiralty. The German pocket battleship *Graf Spee* had spent the first three months of the war roaming at will around the Atlantic and Indian Oceans preying on British merchant ships, sinking nine, and in the process tying up a sizeable proportion of our own naval forces in their endeavour to put an end to her activities. At last, on 13 December, Force G under Commodore Harwood, consisting of three cruisers, the *Exeter*, *Ajax* and *Achilles*, intercepted the *Graf Spee* off the mouth of the River Plate in South America and engaged her. The battle itself was indecisive, but caused the German Captain Langsdorff to seek shelter in the neutral port of Montevideo to carry out repairs. Finally given an ultimatum by the Uruguayans to leave or be interned and believing, quite wrongly, that a battleship and aircraft-carriers had joined the waiting cruisers, Langsdorff telegraphed Germany for instructions. The reply, reputedly from Hitler himself, was that *Graf Spee* should be scuttled. The order was carried out on the evening of 17 December, just beyond the three-mile limit, and the raider's tragic commander shot himself two days later.

It was in 1958, while stationed at HMS *Collingwood*, that I first learned of a song about the Battle of the River Plate. A Liverpool friend told me he had once heard it sung by some drunken reveller on a late-night bus in that city. This was enough to set my quest in motion, but it was a full twenty-five years before such a song came into my possession:

64 *The Battle of the River Plate*
(Tune: 'South of the Border')

South of the border,
Down Montvedeo way,
That's where the pocket battleship
Graf Spee came out one day,
To sink innocent merchantmen
Who were on their way
South of the border,
Down River Plate way.

Now Captain Langsdorff thought:
'*Formose* easy prey.'
Oh but he did not know
That for him it was the day.
For over the skyline
Came steaming that way
Three British cruisers
To keep him at bay.

Now Jerry smiled when the eleven inch started.
For he thought the fight would soon be over.

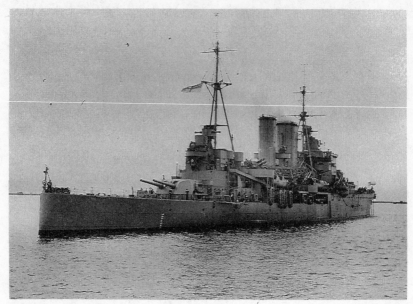

HMS *Exeter*

But the *Exeter* she dashed in light-hearted,
Although outgunned in every way.

Then came the *Ajax*
And the *Achilles* as well,
And what they done to that Hun
History will surely tell.
For eighteen long hours
They fought her like hell,
Made her a pack-it-up battleship,
It was her death knell.

From the British Navy
She started to run
Way up the River Plate, it was the fate
Of this Naval Hun.
For the Uruguayans told her
That she mustn't stay
More than seventy-two hours
In Montvedeo Bay.

84

To her inglorious end
They took her that night,
For Hitler told them to scuttle her,
For they dare not fight.
Whilst the British White Ensign
It flows proud and free
South of the Border
And on every sea.

So Jack Ahoy
Keep the flag on high.
The Nelson Spirit
Will never die.

'*Montvedeo*': This corruption of 'Montevideo' was apparently necessary for the purposes of scansion.

Another song on this action, 'The Sinking of the *Graf Spee*', was collected in Portadown, Northern Ireland, by Robin Morton and published by him in *Folk Songs Sung in Ulster* (Mercier Press, Cork, 1970), but although given generous permission to reproduce this excellent composition I have reluctantly excluded it from this collection as I have no evidence that it ever had any oral currency in the Royal Navy itself. Incidentally both songs refer to three 'British' cruisers, when in fact the *Achilles* belonged to the Royal New Zealand Navy. Furthermore, the action fought between the cruisers and the German battleship lasted for an hour and a half, not eighteen hours as the song says.

A similar one-man song-hunt was sparked off after I heard an incoherent imbiber shambling his way through what was apparently a narrative of the *Jervis Bay* action late one night in a now-demolished pub in King Street, Plymouth, some time around 1960–1. The singer was a vagrant staying at the nearby hostel, and at closing-time I arranged to meet him back at the pub the following lunch-time, when I hoped his head would be a bit clearer, to get a proper rendering of the song. He failed to keep the rendezous, and to my intense disappointment I discovered at the hostel that he had moved on to pastures unknown. I am happy to say that, although I had to wait many years before I encountered the song again, persistence brought results, and in the course of time several versions came my way.

The gallant action of 5 November 1940, in which the 14,000-ton armed merchant ship *Jervis Bay* under Captain Fogarty Fegen engaged the German pocket battleship *Admiral Scheer* in order to give Atlantic convoy HX 84 time to scatter, has deservedly entered the annals of great sea heroism. By steaming straight at the enemy with guns blazing and taking the full fire of the German eleven-inch guns and secondary armament for twenty-two minutes before finally sinking, the *Jervis Bay* enabled 32 of the 37 merchantmen to escape in the encroaching darkness, limiting the *Scheer*'s tally to a mere 5. No fewer than three-quarters of the *Jervis Bay*'s crew of 254 lost their lives, including Captain Fegen, who was awarded a posthumous VC.

The song is performed in either of two ways. When the tune of the Australian song 'Suvla Bay' is used an adaptation of that song's chorus is added after each verse or at the end of the song. Alternatively, the tune of the Irish 'Kevin Barry', in other words the old sea song 'Rolling Home', is used, in which case a chorus is dispensed with. In the composite version that follows I have opted for the 'Suvla Bay' form.

65 The 'Jervis Bay'

'Twas a bleak November evening
With a convoy on its way,
When the look-out spied a raider
From the bridge of *Jervis Bay*.
'Clear the decks for action'
Was the order of the day
As the gallant Captain Fegen
Steered his ship into the fray.

Chorus
Why do I weep, why do I pray?
My love's asleep so far away.
He played his part that Autumn day,
And now he sleeps in *Jervis Bay*.

'Scatter' he told the convoy.
Each ship went a different way
As the *Scheer* fired her first broadside
At the gallant Jervis Bay.

86

She was only a merchant cruiser
Up against a battleship,
But she took that noble action
Just to let the convoy slip.

Outgunned and outranged
She steamed towards the prey.
Each man stood to his station
On the decks of the *Jervis Bay*.
Shells crashed all about her
As she went to bar the way,
To gain time for the convoy,
Oh so brave, the *Jervis Bay*.

Hopeless were the odds,
Men knelt down to pray.
The British guns they roared defiant
From the decks of the *Jervis Bay*.
Men everywhere were dying,
Battered and half sunk she lay
Yet still shells hit the German
From the guns of the *Jervis Bay*.

On the decks lay dead and dying,
And for them the fight was done,
But as the convoy scattered
Then they knew their battle won.
And now the story's over,
And for many a live-long day
Men will talk of the merchant cruiser
That was the *Jervis Bay*.

A peculiarity of the *Jervis Bay* song is that in the opening line it is more common to find the month given as September rather than November, and the time of day as morning rather than evening. The *Jervis Bay* first sighted the *Admiral Scheer* at 16.45 hours.

In the opening stages of the Battle of the River Plate HMS *Exeter* had suffered severely from the virtually undivided attention of the *Graf Spee*'s eleven-inch guns. Her bridge was wrecked, all turrets put out of action and, with sixty-four of her crew killed, she had limped off to the Falkland Islands for repairs. By the time of our next song, however, she was obviously back in full fighting trim. According to my informant the piece originated with two of her stokers in 1941, and he goes on:

> Now this song was written when we were on patrol off Iceland and in the Denmark Strait, and I think you will agree that it was truly prophetic. I often thought of these words later, as we were sunk by the Japanese in the Java Sea and finished up POW's in the Land of the Rising Sun.

66 HMS 'Exeter' Song
(Tune: 'Bless 'Em All')

When the *Exeter* went on patrol
We all put our woollies on,
But South of the Border is more in our line,
Or the Land of the Rising Sun.
There were HO's and PO's and stroppy OD's
Who'd answered their country's call,
But a certain marine down the fore magazine
Said, 'Duet mon droit, bless 'em all.'

Of all the triumphs and tragedies that went to make up the Battle of the Atlantic, as it became known, none could have left a more bitter-sweet aftertaste for both Britain and Germany than the hunting down and eventual destruction of the powerful new super-battleship *Bismark*. When at 10.36 a.m. on 27 May 1941, HMS *Dorsetshire* delivered the *coup de grâce* with a torpedo in either flank of the blazing, shell-torn leviathan, the Royal Navy and the British nation as a whole could be forgiven a feeling of deep satisfaction at the realisation that, just like her predecessors *Good Hope* and *Monmouth* in 1914, HMS *Hood* had been avenged in the fullest and most equitable manner imaginable. Three days previously, early on the morning of 24 May, the *Bismark* had turned a gunner's dream into stark and horrific reality by scoring a direct hit on the after magazines of the magnificent, though out-of-date, pride of the British Fleet, blowing this writer's uncle and 1,415 of his shipmates to oblivion and, in less than two minutes, removing from the surface waters of the Denmark Strait all visible trace of Admiral Holland's noble flagship.

The *Bismark* and *Prinz Eugen* then turned their combined attention upon HMS *Prince of Wales*, which was soon forced to retire from the action. The song that went the rounds soon after implied that she was involved in the subsequent chasing and sinking of the *Bismark*, but in fact events beyond her control carried the action away from her and she withdrew to Iceland to patch up her wounds. According to one crew member her reception was not all it should have been:

> We steamed back to Iceland for repairs after that, and a lot of fights broke out between our crew and men from other ships. They thought we had run off and left the *Hood* to get blown up. But nobody could have prevented that.
>
> (Plymouth *Independent*, 11 October 1970)

In fact, for a brand-new ship not yet fully worked up, with dockyard personnel still aboard tackling many gunnery snags, *Prince of Wales* had acquitted herself as well as could be expected.

67 *The Sinking of HMS 'Hood'*
(Tune: 'Silent Night')

When HMS *Hood* went down in the deep
That was the news that made most mothers weep,
For their sons who had fought for their country so proud
Lie deep down below with the sea for a shroud.
They're sleeping in heavenly peace,
Sleeping in heavenly peace.

Then came the day with her guns in full play
The *Hood* she was sunk that sad day in May.
They had a duty which they had to do,
We are still proud of the Red, White and Blue,
But for our boys we are sad,
Yes for our boys we are sad.

It was *King George the Fifth*, the *Prince of Wales* too,
They took in hand what the *Hood* had to do,
The *Norfolk*, the *Suffolk*, *Dorsetshire* as well,
Along with the *Rodney* sent *Bismark* to hell.
Now the seas are clear, all is well,
We're proud of our Navy so swell.

So mothers and wives and sweethearts be proud,
Though your boys lie below with the sea for a shroud
They were fighting for freedom, let's never forget,
For us to be British, and British we're yet.
They're sleeping in heavenly peace,
Sleeping in heavenly peace.

It has been pointed out that like every other major engagement
fought by the Royal Navy in the Second World War the action
against the *Bismark* was the result of an essential need to protect
merchant ships. To begin with it was the safety of the Atlantic
convoys that caused greatest concern, but from the summer of 1941
onwards the maintaining of strategic supplies to our Russian allies
involved the organisation of regular convoys running from Iceland to
Murmansk or Archangel, a route the major part of which lay within
easy reach of the German air and naval bases in occupied Norway and
Finland. The task of protecting these unarmed vessels from round-
the-clock harassment by U-boats, surface forces and the Luftwaffe,
often in mountainous seas and pitiless sub-zero temperatures,
stretched the resources of the Royal Navy, in terms of both ships and
men, to the utmost limits. If their songs are anything to go by, the
men reacted in the two-fold fashion customary with the British. On
the one hand they sought to ease the protracted misery of endless
hours at action-stations by native recourse to flippancy:

68 *Russian Convoy Escort's Song*
(Tune: 'The Twelve Days of Christmas')

The first day from Iceland old AC-IC said to me
There's a Whitley up a gum tree.

The second day from Iceland old AC-IC said to me
Two Blohm and Voss
And a Whitley up a gum tree.

The third day from Iceland old AC-IC said to me
Three Fokke-Wulfs, two Blohm and Voss
And a Whitley up a gum tree.

The fourth day from Iceland old AC-IC said to me

Four Eighty-eights, three Fokke-Wulfs, two Blohm and Voss
And a Whitley up a gum tree.

The fifth day from Iceland old AC-IC said to me
Five ruddy great bombs, four Eighty-eights,
Three Fokke-Wulfs, two Blohm and Voss
And a Whitley up a gum tree.

The sixth day from Iceland old AC-IC said to me
Six Heinkels dropping five ruddy great bombs,
Four Eighty-eights, three Fokke-Wulfs, two Blohm and Voss
And a Whitley up a gum tree.

The seventh day from Iceland old AC-IC said to me
Seven merchantmen sinking, six Heinkels dropping
Five ruddy great bombs, four Eighty-eights,
Three Fokke-Wulfs, two Blohm and Voss
And a Whitley up a gum tree.

The eighth day from Iceland old AC-IC said to me
Eight U-boats strafing, seven merchantmen sinking,
Six Heinkels dropping five ruddy great bombs,
Four Eighty-eights, three Fokke-Wulfs, two Blohm and Voss
And a Whitley up a gum tree.

The ninth day from Iceland old AC-IC said to me
Nine destroyers hunting, eight U-boats strafing,
Seven merchantmen sinking, six Heinkels dropping
Five ruddy great bombs, four Eighty-eights,
Three Fokke-Wulfs, two Blohm and Voss
And a Whitley up a gum tree.

The tenth day from Iceland old AC-IC said to me
Ten Captains driving nine destroyers hunting,
Eight U-boats strafing, seven merchantmen sinking,
Six Heinkels dropping five ruddy great bombs,
Four Eighty-eights, three Fokke-Wulfs, two Blohm and Voss
And a Whitley up a gum tree.

On the other hand the desire to 'tell it like it was' led to lyrics of protest that were far from flippant. And, more surprisingly, it was not just the lower-deck grousers who unleashed their feelings on the icy Arctic air. The next song, without a doubt the finest the Royal Navy produced in the Second World War and a worthy rival of the Army's 'D-Day Dodgers', was launched by a group of officers on various destroyers of the 23rd Flotilla but it soon passed into the oral tradition of both wardroom and messdeck alike. The originator, it seems, was Captain C. J. ('Jock') Cunningham DSC RN, at that time First Lieutenant of HMS *Savage*, ably assisted, so he told me, by Lieutenant Dickie Birks RCNVR. He described the song's genesis as follows:

> In those days the First Lieutenant traditionally kept the morning watch (0400–0800) and first dog-watch (1600–1800) – maybe the tradition still holds good. Anyway Dickie, as Second Officer-of-the-Watch, and I cobbled the thing together with me on the bridge in contact via the standard Admiralty pattern voice-pipe to him in the wheelhouse/plot below, where dim red light was available to see what he was writing, and in this manner the 23rd D.F. song was born and many seemingly tedious and rather chilly hours were shortened. Obviously, once started, many others contributed, not least signalmen and, indeed, bridge look-outs.
>
> It did create a sense of unity and 'we'll beat the bastards', and I well remember our libertymen having to be recalled from an anticipated evening ashore at the destroyer canteen in Scapa, after a bare hour, due to sudden sailing orders. They marched themselves immaculately in full voice to the jetty and continued to sing in the drifter until alongside.

The second line is pure sarcasm, of course. The enemy-held airfield at Petsamo, on the cramped coastline of northern Finland, was a bare sixty miles from Kola Inlet itself, which brought the hapless merchantmen and their escorts within even easier range during the final stage of their voyage.

69 *Twenty-third Flotilla Song*
(Tune: 'Lili Marlene')

Up to Kola Inlet, back to Scapa Flow,
Soon we shall be calling for oil at Petsamo.
Why does it always seem to be
Flotilla number twenty-three

Up to the Arctic Ocean,
Up to the Barents Sea?

When we get to Scapa do we get a rest?
All we get are signals invariably addressed:
Savage, Scorpion, from your Com. (D),
'What brings you here? Get back to sea,
Back to the Arctic Ocean,
Back to the Barents Sea.'

Now and then we get a slightly different job,
But it's always screening around the same old mob,
Watching the 'A' boys prang the Hun
With never a chance to fire the quarter gun,
Up in the Arctic Ocean,
Up in the Barents Sea.

Once we lay in harbour, swinging round the buoy,
Waiting for the drifter, but still there was no joy.
In came the signal, 'Weigh, proceed,
'At your best speed, great is your need
'Up in the Arctic Ocean,
'Up in the Barents Sea.'

Over in our mileage, due for boiler-clean,
When we're not with convoys there's shooting in between.
Now as you have surely guessed
We do our best, but need a rest
Out of the Arctic Ocean,
Out of the Barents Sea.

Battleships and cruisers lying round in state,
Watching poor destroyers sail out Switha gate.
They're the ships the papers call 'The Fleet',
They look so neat, but have no beat
Up in the Arctic Ocean,
Up in the Barents Sea.

What it is to have a crazy Number One,
All the boys are chokker although they've just begun.
The wretched Pilot sits and drinks,
The Captain thinks, the whole thing stinks,
We hate the Arctic Ocean,
We hate the Barents Sea.

There is at least one further stanza, which I am afraid I do not have in its entirety. I have also been told that other verses were dropped because their sentiments were anti-Russian, but I have been unable to verify this. It seems unlikely that Jack would allow himself to be dictated to in matters of singing.

The envy felt by crews of smaller warships as they sailed past 'Battleships and cruisers lying round in state' every time they left or entered harbour was probably universal and not limited to Arctic convoys. By their very existence capital ships were natural headline-stealers, whereas it needed either a special escapade or a special commander, as with the cases of HMS *Cossack* and *Kelly*, before the more menial elements of the fleet caught the public's attention:

70 *Little Ships*
(Tune: 'The Little Boy that Santa Claus Forgot')

They're the little ships that Winston Churchill forgot,
And he didn't know when one of those got lost.
He'd not forget the *Rodney*, the *Nelson* or the *Hood*.
These little ships of ours are doing all they ever could.
And as they take the convoys to and fro
And journey back to dear old Blighty's shore,
I'm sorry for those ships dear,
They've had a hell of a blitz dear,
They're the little ships that Winston Churchill forgot.

There is no doubt that in the first and last lines 'Winston C.' would scan better than 'Winston Churchill', but I have no evidence that it was ever sung that way.

Among many heroic tasks undertaken by these little ships the work of minesweepers deserves special mention. To be fully aware that the patch of water ahead has been liberally strewn with concealed high-explosive, yet nevertheless to nose your way through it with the express intent of rendering the area safe by deliberate detonation, so starkly described by 'Bartimeus' in 1917 as 'setting forth in the comfortless dawn to holystone Death's doorstep', was a way of life that called for the coolness of a matador and the nerve of a steeplejack. A certain measure of sanguine humour, too, did not come amiss:

'We're dodging mines, dodging mines'

71 Sweepers

We're dodging mines, dodging mines,
Always bleeding well dodging mines.
There's one just over here,
Another one over there,
There's one just off the quarterdeck,
My God they're everywhere.
We're dodging mines, dodging mines,
Always bleeding well dodging mines.
There's one over there as black as coal,
I'd love to shove it up Hitler's hole,
We're always bleeding well dodging mines.

At the personal level there were certain categories of sailors who, like the little ships, found themselves short-changed by a poorly-informed public, and often suffered the mortification of finding their worthy wartime role pitifully underrated. Had a Sick Berth Attendant (SBA), the medical orderly of the Service, been dressed in 'square rig' like other Jack Tars the appropriate gratitude and esteem of shore-dwellers would have been his for the asking. As it was, with his black peaked cap, modest red cap-badge and sober black buttons inconspicuous on a dark, double-breasted jacket, he stood a better chance, especially beyond Naval port areas, of being mistaken for some colourless non-combatant:

72 SBA's Song
(Tune: 'Broken Doll')

As I walked down the street the other day
A lady came to me and she did say:
'Why aren't you in khaki or Air Force blue,
'Fighting for your country like the other fellows do?'
I turned to her and tears came to my eyes.
I said, 'Now lady, don't you realise?
'I'm not a taxi-driver, I'm an SBA,
'A *S*ailor with a *B*roken '*A*rt.'

In addition to its sterling service on warships and in Royal Naval Hospitals the medical branch formed a much larger proportion of the ship's company aboard Hospital Ships, where, unlike their colleagues on grey-funnelled men-of-war they could at least enjoy the modest luxury of sailing on a fully-lit ship at night, as we hear in our final wartime song, a favourite aboard the Hospital Ship *Maine* in the Mediterranean:

73 Hospital Ship Song
(Tune: 'Mountains of Mourne')

Oh messmates the *Maine* is a wonderful sight
When she steams out of Alex. with lamps on at night.
We know where we're bound for and where we will go,
The felucca wog told us, and he ought to know.
'Your ship's off to Malta,' he said with a smile,
'You can walk on the wrecks there for over a mile.'
We went and we came back, as you can now see,
Tombola at Fleet Club, Britannia for tea.

We chased the Eighth Army on Africa's shore,
And brought back some Jerries and Wops by the score.
We dropped them at Alex. to our relief,
Then cleaned up the wards with an order from Chief.
He said, 'You are free now to make for the shore,
'No Stella beer or your head will be sore.'
We caught the first liberty and made for the quay,
Spent all our akkers, then back off to sea.

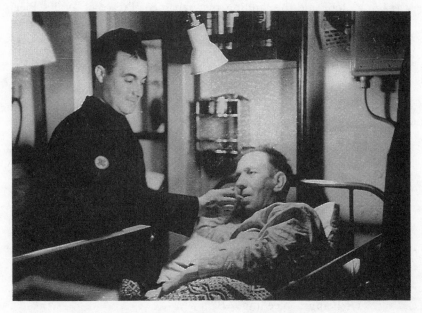

'I'm not a taxi-driver, I'm an SBA'

97

FLEET AIR ARM

Whether or not it will cause naval historians to amend their records, the fact is that many years before the idea occurred to anyone at the Admiralty, what was to become known as the Fleet Air Arm had already been envisaged in song by a humble, anonymous matelot. He was serving on board HMS *Prince of Wales* when she arrived for the first time at Dover in 1909, and it was on 25 July, whilst the ship was lying alongside the landing pier renamed 'Prince of Wales Pier' in her honour, that Louis Blériot flew overhead on his historic channel crossing. Reflecting on the event our unnamed bluejacket, with a vision almost Wellsian in its reach, foresaw the advent of a Royal Navy whose principal strike weapon would be ship-borne aircraft, 'the Aeroplane Navy' as he called it. His only mistake lay in believing that this would bring to an end the life of daily drudgery endured by the plebeian Jack Tar. As he saw it, in this new Utopian Navy the seaman and the stoker would be redundant, and he expressed his yearning for the anticipated day of deliverance in one of the Navy's most poignant songs:

74 *Roll on the Aeroplane Navy*
(Tune: Possibly 'Botany Bay')

I'm sick and tired of the Navy,
Of being a bleeding AB,
And life is no joke when you're bleeding well broke
For a poor little matelot like me.

Oh I'm but a poor Pusser's slavey,
My chances in the Navy are small,
So roll on the Aeroplane Navy,
When they won't want no flatfoots at all.

I'm the man that handles the shovel,
The devil, the ash-rake and slice,
But I think we would be better stokers
If they served us out chopsticks and rice.
Oh I'm but a poor Pusser's slavey,
My chances in the Navy are small,
So roll on the Aeroplane Navy,
When they won't want no dustmen at all.

Even if his prediction regarding the consequences of naval aviation
had turned out to be blissfully accurate this songman-visionary would
have had a long wait for its fulfilment. Four years were to go by
before a seaplane-carrier, HMS *Hermes*, was introduced, and the first
aircraft-carrier proper, HMS *Argus*, did not make its appearance until

'I'm the man that handles the shovel,
The devil, the ash-rake and slice'

1917. Paradoxically, then, the earliest 'Fleet Air Arm' ditty not only dates from well before the Branch even existed (though trying to determine exactly when today's Fleet Air Arm can claim to have begun would make an absorbing diversion for a rainy long weekend), but it is even older than the Royal Naval Air Service songs made up at the Western Front during the 1914–18 war (see *The Airman's Song Book*, edited by C. H. Ward-Jackson and Leighton Lucas, William Blackwood & Sons, 1967).

Not surprisingly, a sizeable part of the Fleet Air Arm repertoire is concerned with deck landings. The technique was tricky and demanding, and accidents were plentiful, even more so in wartime when the approaching aircraft could already be severely damaged. Films and television must by now have familiarised the lay public with the paraphernalia of the operation: the 'batsman' (Deck Landing Officer) with his own brand of tick-tack telegraphy telling the pilot to go higher or lower, to alter his speed or make another approach, the aircraft hook engaging in the arrester wires across the flight deck, and the crash barriers into which it was hoped the aircraft would plunge if the arrester wires were missed. Much less well known were the little platform at the after end of the 'island' or superstructure which provided the best vantage point from which to watch the proceedings, known to the pilots as the 'Goofers' Gallery' or 'Goofers' for short, and the accident report form, or A25, which had to be completed in detail by any pilot lucky enough to survive a 'prang'.

'The A25 Song', the unchallenged 'anthem' of the Fleet Air Arm, seems to have begun life in the early years of the Second World War, when the prospect of risking one's life in the face of both a violent foe and a vagarious flight deck was quite enough to bear, without the irony of having to explain in writing, in the middle of a war, why one's aircraft was not in one piece. Like 'Cosher Bailey' and 'The Ball of Kirriemuir' before it, 'The A25 Song' accumulated verses steadily with the passing of the years until eventually the principal theme of deck landings was abandoned in favour of other escapades and topics.

75 *The A25 Song*
(Tune: 'Villikins and his Dinah')

They say in the Air Force a landing's OK
If the pilot gets out and can still walk away,

But in the Fleet Air Arm the prospect is grim
If the landing's piss-poor and the pilot can't swim.

Chorus
Cracking show, I'm alive,
But I still have to render my A25.

I fly for a living and not just for fun,
I'm not very anxious to hack down a Hun,
And as for deck landings at night in the dark,
As I told Wings this morning, 'Blow that for a lark.'

Cracking show, I'm alive,
But I still have to render my A25.

When the batsman gives 'lower' I always go higher,
I drift o'er to starboard and prang my Seafire.
The boys in the 'Goofers' all think that I'm green,
But I get a commission from Supermarine.

Cracking show, I'm alive,
But I still have to render my A25.

They gave me a Barra. to beat up the Fleet,
I shot up the *Rodney* and *Nelson* a treat,
I forgot the high mast that sticks out from *Formid*.
And a seat in the 'Goofers' was worth fifty quid.

'I drift o'er to starboard and prang my Seafire'

Cracking show, I'm alive,
But I still have to render my A25.

I thought I was coming in high enough but
I was fifty feet up when the batsman gave 'cut',
And loud in my earphones the sweet angels sang:
'Float, float, float, float, float, float, float, float, float, float,
   PRANG!'

Cracking show, I'm alive,
But I still have to render my A25.

When you come o'er the round-down and see Wings' frown
You can safely assume that your hook isn't down.
A dirty great barrier looms up in front,
And you hear Wings shout, 'Switch off your engine, you fool!'

Cracking show, I'm alive,
But I still have to render my A25.

The Wings of St Merryn in a 'Reliant' one day
Set out for Trelliga for tea for to stay,
But as he got there his engine cut out,
And now all you hear is Wings' painful shout:

Cracking show, I'm alive,
But I still have to render my A25.

I swing down the deck in my Martlet Mark Four,
Loud in my ear-'oles the Cyclone's smooth roar:
'*Chuff*-clank-clank, *chuff*-clank-clank, *chuff*-clank-clank-clink!'
Away wing on pom-pom, away life in Drink

Cracking show, I'm alive,
But I still have to render my A25.

I flew over Jay-pan in my F.O.2
Taking some pictures admiring the view,
When up came the flack and I turned round about,
And that's why I sit in my dinghy and shout:

Cracking show, I'm alive,
But I still have to render my A25.

I came back to England and much to my wrath
They gave me some dual in an old Tiger Moth,
Which does fifty-five knots or something fantastic,
Which is bloody good-o on some string and elastic.

Cracking show, I'm alive,
But I still have to render my A25.

One night in the Wardroom a subby named Bash,
An awkward young bastard with a ginger moustache,
Said, 'Chaps I must drown all my sorrows in gin,
'I've been twelve hours ashore and I can't get it in.'

Cracking show, I'm alive,
But I still have to render my A25.

I sat in the starter awaiting the kick,
Amusing myself by rotating the stick.
Down came the green flag, the plane gave a cough,
'Gor Blimey,' said Wings, 'he has tossed himself off!'

Cracking show, I'm alive,
But I still have to render my A25.

Now in the Luftwaffe they never complain
Since Goering invented the pilotless plane.
They sit in the crew room and sing all the day,
And this is the song that they sing so they say:

Cracking show, I'm alive,
But I still have to render my A25.

The moral of this story is easy to see,
A Fleet Air Arm pilot you never should be,
But stay on the shore and get two rings or three,
And go out every night on the piss down at Lee.

Cracking show, I'm alive,
But I still have to render my A25.

It is customary for the rhyme set up for the end of verse six to remain
unfulfilled, presumably because singers have discovered that a bigger laugh
ensues when a milder epithet is substituted for the obvious one.

Another song, involving not only the evils of deck-landing but also the rivalry and leg-pulling that existed between the Royal Navy pilots and their hostilities-only counterparts from civvy-street, the Royal Naval Volunteer Reserve pilots, was the following. Judging by the place names in the sixth verse it must have been current among fliers who had been stationed in the Orkneys.

76 *There's a Fuck-up on the Flight Deck*
(Tune: Based on 'The Hut Sut Sung')

Chorus:
There's a fuck-up on the flight deck and the Wavy Navy done it,
There's a prang on the gangway and they don't know who to blame.

Verse:
The 'K.G. Five's' ten miles astern, and she should be five ahead,
But the screwy turn by a 'makee-learn' reads 'blue' instead of 'red'.

Chorus: There's a fuck-up on the flight deck, etc.

Ten Albacores were neatly ranged to bomb and blitz Bodo,
Commander (F) was sold a pup, 'cos seven didn't go.

Chorus: There's a fuck-up, etc.

The Safety Boat'll no longer float, the Cox'n can't be found,
The cutter's prow has hit the brow and the Bosun's Mate's been
    drowned.

Chorus: There's a fuck-up, etc.

Like bats from hell come the lads pell mell, each flying fit to burst,
It's time for lunch and the whole darn bunch is trying to land on
    first.

Chorus: There's a fuck-up, etc.

Reds galore from an Albacore nosediving for the drink,
'Di-da, di-da' comes from afar as a Fulmar starts to sink.

Chorus: There's a fuck-up, etc.

Commander (F) was on the bridge, leaning against the rail,
Discussing dirt and bits of skirt from Hatston, Twatt and Crail.

Chorus: There's a fuck-up, etc.

An Albacore came in to land and pranged into a barrier.
These RN types are quite all right, but they're no bloody good on a
carrier.

Alternative:
A solitary straight 'A' said to Wings as the first one hit the barrier:
'By gosh, these H.O's may wear rings but they're damn all use in a
carrier.'

Chorus: There's a fuck-up, etc.

The "K.G. Five": HMS 'King George V'.
Makee-learn: A young RN midshipman training as a navigator.
Blue, red: Local fleet codes, changed regularly.
Reds galore: When an aircraft 'ditched' in the sea the normal procedure was
for red flares from a Very pistol to be fired to indicate the number of men
alive; one flare for each man.
Di-da, di-da: Probably WT which operated automatically on contact with
water. Fitted as standard equipment in later dinghies.
Straight 'A': It seems this principally referred to the order that sometimes
had to be given when an aircraft 'pranged' whilst attempting a flight deck
landing, 'Maintain speed and course for existing aircraft to land on', but
here it looks as if the term has been transferred to a pilot RN, who would
wear on his sleeve a 'straight' ring, as distinct from the 'wavy' ring of an
RNVR officer, with the letter 'A' in the loop.

For most of the inter-war years the Fleet Air Arm had existed
under a very uneasy system of dual control, with the RAF responsible
for its administration as well as the design and construction of its
aircraft. When, shortly before the Second World War, the Admiralty
finally wrested total control of its aviation branch away from the Air
Ministry, it found itself, for a variety of reasons, left with a legacy of
largely obsolete aircraft. Nevertheless, the exploits of the torpedo-
carrying Fairey Swordfish and their gallant crews throughout the first
half of the Second World War provided the naval air branch with the
most glorious chapters in its short history. No wonder those who
survived could look back with such nostalgia and pride:

77 *How Lovely it Was*
(Tune: 'Thanks for the Memory')

Thanks for the memory
Of biplanes in the sky,
Of pilots who could fly,
Of four-hour trips
Attacking ships,
Returning with a sigh,
How lovely it was.

And thanks for the memory
Of drunken nights ashore,
Of blacks put up galore,
Of gin and lime
And flying time
And popsies by the score,
How lovely it was.

Many's the time that we've pranged 'em
On many an ALT,
And many's the time we've stranged 'em,
No ASV, no WT.

Thanks for the memory
Of large fixed under-carts,
Of evenings playing darts,
Of Wrens galore
When we're ashore
And lots of broken hearts,
We thank you, so much.

The verb 'stranged' seems to be a nonsense word used in desperation for a rhyme.

We have seen earlier, with 'Shotley Stew' (No. 31) and 'The *Raleigh* Song' (No. 37), that training establishments had a repertoire peculiar to themselves, and the Fleet Air Arm was no exception. Like the *Raleigh* boys, the inmates of HMS *Ariel*, the radio/radar training school of the Royal Naval Air Service at Worthy Down, Hampshire, felt under some kind of banishment, and around 1950 they could be heard singing:

78 HMS 'Ariel' Song
(Tune: 'Serenade No.1' by Heykens)

Air-i-el,
Shades of Hell,
What a place to live in.
Rain all round,
Weather bound,
Gone to ground and never be found
For years and years,
Confirms our fears
That we're forgotten numbers.
Here are we till eternity
While the FOGT slumbers.

To conclude this section here are two pieces from the party repertoire of members of 802 Squadron serving on board HMS *Theseus* during the period 1953-4. Neither can be classed as a song, both being recited or chanted. Both, too, are modelled on well tried formulae. The 23rd Psalm, so often the vehicle of parody, is the basis of this tongue-in-cheek tribute to the indispensable Deck Landing Officer:

79 Irreverence

The Batsman is my shepherd, I shall not crash.
He maketh me to land on flat runways.
He bringeth me in off rough waters.
He restoreth my confidence.
Yea, though I come stalling into the deck at sixty knots
I shall fear no evil,
For he is with me.
His arms and his bats they comfort me.
He prepareth a deck before me in the presence of mine enemies.
He attacheth my hook to the wire.
My deck space runneth over.

Mine enemies: The Goofers' Gallery (See 'The A25 Song', No. 75).

'The Batsman is my shepherd, I shall not crash'

Even more parodied than the 23rd Psalm is the old English nursery rhyme 'Ten Little Nigger Boys'. There are at least three distinct examples associated with the Royal Navy, including this offering from the *Theseus* lads:

80 *Ten Little Furies*

Ten little Furies, landing on so fine.
One hit the round-down, Ting! Bang! Nine!

Nine little Furies, one straightened out too late,
Three inches armoured deck. Only eight!

Eight little Furies, climbing up to heaven.
Who's whipped me blasted oxygen? That leaves seven!

Seven little Furies, one asked for a fix.
Controller's busy in the mess. That leaves six!

'Nine little Furies, one straightened out too late'

Six little Furies made a formation dive.
One forgot his airbrakes. Then there were five!

Five little Furies, beating up the tower.
One did a smashing job. Now there's only 'fower'!

Four little Furies, a long way out to sea.
One hadn't topped up his tanks. Now we've only three!

Three little Furies, feeling very few.
The Bofors wanted practice. That left just two!

Two little Furies, playing with a camera gun.
Tried to blackmail the Captain's wife. That left just one!

One little Fury, being flown by Number One.
Sugar in his petrol tanks. GOOD IDEA SON!

Asked for a fix: In view of the different construction this term has acquired since the early 1950s it is as well to point out that the meaning here is to request clarification of the aircraft's geographical position.

SUBMARINES

Their respective operational elements could hardly present a greater contrast, yet there are some obvious parallels between the subjects of this section and the previous one. Like their opposite numbers in the Fleet Air Arm, submariners are a brotherhood with but the briefest of pedigrees.

As viable branches of the British Navy they were both undreamed of even when the first ironclad battleships were already gliding down Victorian slipways. And, as with their colleagues in naval aviation, the outbreak of war merely intensified the tang of danger that constantly permeated even their peacetime undertakings. Yet their songs, again like those of the flying fraternity, seem to encourage the axiom that the greater the peril the lighter the muse.

For instance, no class of submarine was more disaster-prone than the revolutionary 'K' Class. Steam-driven on the surface, with a maximum speed of 25 knots, retractable funnels and a diving time of four minutes, these cumbrous monsters needed no war to put them on speaking terms with calamity, although seventeen were commissioned between August 1916 and May 1918.

Disastrous experiments they may have been, but they seem to have been manned by a bunch of light-hearted optimists. The last steam-driven 'K'-boat, *K26*, was commissioned as late as May 1923, and four years later in a Maltese creek her crew, painting the casing in preparation for an inspection by Sir Roger Keyes, could be heard singing:

81 The K26 Song
(Tune: 'It Ain't Gonna Rain No More')

K26 is a bloody fine boat,
Her casing's painted white,
She works her crew all through the day
And half the bleeding night.

"Jimmy" heard it,' one of them remembered, 'and, having a good sense of humour, worked us till supper time.'

When I look back on my own service in submarines one feature stands out from all the rest, and that is the lack of proper sleep. In 'boats' war spills over into peace. Set aside the fear and danger of the former and 'Patrol Routine' is much the same, a sour-tasting layer-cake of slumbering consciousness and half-conscious slumber. The irritating regularity with which dreams were dispelled by the urgent hand of the shaker, the subtle insistence of the night alarm or the jackboot brutality of the klaxon robbed day and night of their distinction, and no song evokes the experience of this protracted torment more than the following parody. The submariner was astute enough to choose a weary-sounding melody made famous by Flanagan and Allen in 1932, and the presence here of the tune's 'verse', or introduction, in addition to the well-known 'chorus' suggests that the underwater version was put together hot on the heels of the original, which it follows very closely.

82 Underneath the Surface
(Tune: 'Underneath the Arches')

Big ships we never cared for,
Destroyers they can keep.
There is only one place that we know,
That is deep down deep.

Chorus
Underneath the surface
We dream our dreams away.
Underneath the surface
On battery-boards we lay.

111

There you'll always find us,
Tired out and worn,
Waiting for the coxswain to wake us
With the sound of the klaxon horn.
Then we all get busy,
The tiffies and the 'swains,
Working vents and blows and hydroplanes,
And when the panic's over
We'll get it down again.
Underneath the surface
We dream our dreams away.

With all ranks living at close quarters, relationships between the men and their superiors, if perhaps not always as egalitarian as popularly supposed, were graced with a touch more empathy and benevolence (upwards as well as downwards) than was usually to be found in the compartmentalised world of the surface man-of-war. For instance, although among the many duties of the Coxswain were

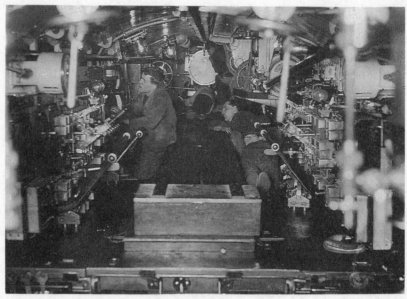

'Underneath the surface
We dream our dreams away'

those carried out by the Master-at-Arms in larger ships and establishments his was seldom the 'bogeyman' image associated with the 'Jaunty'. Certainly not, at any rate, on one submarine on which I served, where our Coxswain, in storing ship for a short spell at sea, completely overlooked the rum ration yet somehow managed to remain as popular as ever. And apparently not, either, on the *Starfish* in the China Seas just before the Second World War:

83 The 'Starfish' Song
(Tune: 'They're Tough, Mighty Tough, in the West')

Oh we're tough, mighty tough, in *Starfish*,
And the Coxswain is a man that we well wish.
Oh the cook makes hors-de-overs
Out of matelot's old pullovers.
Oh we're tough, mighty tough, in *Starfish*.

Alas, when hostilities broke out poor *Starfish* became one of many British submarines whose war turned out to be dramatically short. She was sunk by armed German trawlers near the Heligoland Bight on 9 January 1940, though her crew (including those Far Eastern songsters I wonder?) were fortunately saved. In fact, of the twelve 'S'-Class submarines which began the war only three were left by the end of 1940, the fate of the remainder being chronicled in a typically dispassionate creation popular among contemporary submariners, even those aboard the three survivors, *Sealion, Seawolf* and *Sturgeon* (each of whom were to see the war out):

84 Twelve Little 'S'-Boats

Twelve little 'S'-boats 'go to it' like Bevin,
Starfish goes a bit too far – then there were eleven.

Eleven watchful 'S'-boats doing fine and then
Seahorse fails to answer – so there are ten.

Ten stocky 'S'-boats in a ragged line,
Sterlet stops and drops out – leaving us nine.

'Twelve little "S"-boats'

Nine plucky 'S'-boats, all pursuing fate,
Shark, is overtaken – now we are eight.

Eight sturdy 'S'-boats, men from Hants and Devon,
Salmon now is overdue – so the number's seven.

Seven gallant 'S'-boats, trying all their tricks,
Spearfish tries a newer one – down we come to six.

Six tireless 'S' boats fighting to survive,
No reply from *Swordfish* – so we tally five.

Five scrubby 'S'-boats, patrolling close inshore,
Snapper takes a short cut – now we are four.

Four fearless 'S'-boats, too far out to sea,
Sunfish bombed and scrap-heaped – we are only three.

By the middle of 1943 Britain had lost some 64 submarines. In fact the point had been reached, according to Alastair Mars in his book *Submarines at War 1939-45* (William Kimber, 1971), when the chances of survival for submariners, many of them non-volunteers, were no better than evens, compared with 10 to 1 in favour for the Navy in general. His remarks concerning the remuneration these heroes received for staking their lives against such odds are worth quoting:

Although the British Government were now (1942) responsible for paying Dutch, Norwegian, French, Belgian, Polish and other armed forces, the British men were by far the lowest paid; in some cases the difference was staggering. Most of the submarine ratings in the Mediterranean had 'stood by' the final stages of their submarines' fitting-out in the building yard. They had therefore seen at first hand that even unskilled workmen were being paid five times as much as themselves; whilst the former lived at home with their families at comparatively little risk — and frequently struck for more money. The pay of an able seaman torpedoman, including all submarine allowances, was then about 10/– a day. If he was killed, which was likely, his family would receive about one-third of that amount.

With many of those families homeless through bombing, and desperately short of money, the submariner had sufficient cause for mental anguish, over and above anything arising from his personal combat predicament. Yet still he sang:

85 *Half Ahead Together*
(Tune: 'Arm in Arm Together')

Half ahead together, take her up to thirty feet,
Raise the after periscope while the Captain has a peep.
There's a Jerry cruiser right on the starboard bow.
Let's go up and sink the cow.

86 *Pump, Suck, Blow*
(Tune: 'Serenade No. 1' by Heykens)

Pump, suck, blow,
Here we go,
Diving is a hazard.
Look at him
Catch the trim,
He's a silly bastard
Flood from aft,
Check main vents,

115

> Blow the after shithouse.
> 'Jimmy's' got a bastard on
> And we don't give a toss.

A First Lieutenant's reputation might stand or fall by the speed and expertise with which he 'caught a trim' immediately after the submarine had dived. Delay in stabilising the boat on an even keel at a steady depth was bound to be an extra source of irritation to the commanding officer and to those other crew members involved in the process. For the crew in general, however, far less momentous considerations might go to determine his worth (see No. 81). One wartime submariner recalls:

> One day in Gib. the casing party were painting the ship. We had just arrived from the UK and were still a comparatively new crew, and 'Jimmy' had kept us at it from commissioning at Barrow. Anyway, late in the afternoon it started to rain, and 'Jimmy' dashed for the forehatch. As his head was just disappearing down the hatch he shouted to the Second Coxswain: 'Make and Mend.' The 'Scratch' came out with:

87 *Don't give us a Make and Mend, Sir*

> Don't give us a Make and Mend, sir,
> We might come over faint.
> There's not many 'Jimmies' like you, sir.
> It's a bloody good job there ain't.

How much of a submariner's piece this is I would not care to say. The sentiment was universal and could be used on any RN vessel.

There was one way at least that a submariner could enjoy the best of both worlds, a 'soft number' whereby he could draw his extra submarine pay whilst enjoying the comparative comforts of a shore-based life. On board every Submarine Depot Ship and at every submarine base there was retained a pool of submariners not attached to any particular submarine. They were known as the 'Spare Crew', and from their ranks were drawn emergency replacements in the event of sickness and so on.

Being a member of Spare Crew had its advantages and disadvantages. On the one hand drawing full submarine pay without going to sea was a very attractive prospect, especially for men resident locally. On the other hand there was always the possibility of a sudden draft to an operational submarine, perhaps one about to set off for a lengthy absence, and with such a Sword of Damocles forever poised a married Spare Crew member kissing his wife goodbye in the morning could never be sure where he would find himself at the day's end, or when he would be seeing her again. Such an uncertain existence was not to everyone's liking. The relative predictability of life on an operational submarine, a 'running boat', was often preferred. Plans could at least be made and usually adhered to.

Both points of view are expressed in the next song, a prime favourite of submariners past and present, and one with many variants:

88 *Come to the Spare Crew*
(Tune: 'Come to the Saviour')

Come to the Spare Crew, make no delay,
Come to the Spare Crew, two bob a day.
Sitting on the messdeck, nothing else to do,
Come to the Spare Crew do.

Chorus
Joyful, joyful, will the Spare Crew be
When the boats have all pushed off to sea.
We'll be sitting on the messdeck, nothing else to do,
So come to the Spare Crew do.

Now we don't want your Spare Crew, it ain't no good at all.
We don't want your two bob, stick it on the wall.
We don't want your Wrennery, we leave it all to you,
'Cos we are a sea-boat's crew.

Chorus Joyful, joyful, etc.

Sea-boat's crew: Somewhat misleading. What is meant, I feel sure, is the crew of a 'sea-going boat', i.e. an operational submarine.

We conclude with a submarine ditty of later, post-war vintage.

Among his string of commercial successes following upon the skiffle boom Lonnie Donegan had a hit with a re-working of an old Irish composition, 'None Can Love Like an Irishman'. The title was adjusted to 'Nobody Loves Like an Irishman' and the Donegan version was speedily parodied by subaqueous songsmiths. For their theme they chose to present, in highly exaggerated form, one of the less attractive aspects of their underwater calling. Within the cramped confines of the pre-nuclear submarine the luxuries of bath, shower and laundry had to be forgone. Only the most fundamental ablutions were practicable, but with everyone, literally, in the same boat it was a bearable limitation, and one which never entailed the neglect of essential personal hygiene. Not that this was any deterrent to the humorist in his search for the laughable side of a far from perfect situation:

89 *Nobody Washes in a Submarine*
(Tune: 'Nobody Loves Like an Irishman')

If you join submarines and you've got any pride
You won't use Persil and you won't use Tide.
If you go in the washroom all the boys declare:
'You'd better not take any soap in there.'

Chorus
For I don't give a damn wherever you've been,
Nobody washes in a submarine.

The Navy think we're a crabby clan.
We haven't had a wash since the trip began.
We've been at sea for three weeks or more,
And now we're covered in shit galore.

Our feet are black where they once were pink.
Three blokes already have died of the stink.
We hid them in the fore-ends where they couldn't be seen,
For to throw them in the sea meant they might have got clean.

ONE FROM THE WRENS

90 Mary was a Three-badge Wren
(Tune: 'Yankee Doodle')

Mary was a three-badge Wren,
Her hair was fair and curly.
She joined the Wrens in 1910,
Just thirty years too early.

Though Mary has her bit of fun
She never gets detention.
Her demob. group is number one,
She well deserves her pension.

Mary is a pusser lass,
She wears her 'black-out' undies.
As a glamour girl she wished to pass,
So she changed them Easter Sundays.

She knew her KR's and AI's,
At them she'd never falter,
Until she met a swell GI
Who led her to the altar.

Though she makes love to Bo'sun's Mates,
They are the Navy's he-men,
The ones she most appreciates
Are able-bodied seamen.

So learn by Mary's awful fate,
You Wrens who flirt a trifle.
You may end up a Gunner's mate
And have to clean his rifle.

GI: Gunnery Instructor (see Glossary).

ENVOI

91 The Matelot's Prayer

Now I lay me down to sleep.
I pray my soul the Lord shall keep,
And grant no other sailor take
My shoes and socks before I wake.
But if some poor soul should chance to stray
And try to take these things away
I'LL PUNCH HIS BLEEDING HEAD IN!!!

APPENDICES

Appendix A
TRADITION CONTINUED

In the Introduction it was pointed out that Royal Navy men of the twentieth-century steamship era did not totally reject the repertoire of the 'sticks and string' sailors of earlier times. By way of illustration, this section contains some examples of those older traditional items that survived, for a time at least, into a more modern age. Purists will no doubt compare some of these later texts with their precursors and regard the evidence as confirmation of the ultimate fate of hallowed tradition in a world of mass consumption and readily-available trivia. Looked at another way, though, these examples, few as they may be, can be seen as testifying to the capacity of an older culture to endure, in however debased a condition, side by side with such a host of freshly minted pieces as are presented in the main body of this work.

While using the titles by which modern sailors have known the songs, I have also included in brackets, if appropriate, the older names by which they will be more familiar to the folk song enthusiast.

92 A Matelot and a Pongo
('A Sailor and a Soldier')
(Tune: See Appendix D)

A matelot and a pongo were walking one day,
Said the pongo to the matelot, 'Let's kneel down and pray,
'And if we have one prayer may we also have ten.'
'Let's have a bloody litany,' said the matelot, 'Amen.'

'The first thing we'll pray for, we'll pray for our tot,
'Glorious tot, makes us shit-hot,
'And if we have one tot may we also have ten.'
'May we have a bloody Spirit Room,' said the matelot, 'Amen.'

'And the next thing we'll pray for, we'll pray for our beer,
'Glorious beer, fills us with cheer,
'And if we have one pint may we also have ten.'
'May we have a bloody brewery,' said the matelot, 'Amen.'

'And the next thing we'll pray for, we'll pray for some money,
'Glorious money, buys us more fanny,
'And if we have one pound may we also have ten.'
'May we have the Bank of England,' said the matelot, 'Amen.'

'And the next thing we'll pray for, we'll pray for our wives,
'Glorious wives, pride of our lives,
'And if we have one wife may we also have ten.'
'May we have a bloody harem,' said the matelot, 'Amen.'

'And the next thing we'll pray for, we'll pray for smallee boys,
'Glorious boys, fill us with joys,
'And if we have one boy may we also have ten.'
'May we have a bloody orphanage,' said the matelot, 'Amen.'

'And the last thing we'll pray for, we'll pray for the Queen,
'Glorious Queen, long may she reign,
'And if she has one sprog may she also have ten.'
'May she have a bloody regiment,' said the matelot, 'Amen.'

Suitably adjusted, this is a song to be found in the repertoire of the other Services and could have been included in Appendix B.

93 *Bell-bottom Trousers*
('Rosemary Lane')

I was a serving maid down in Drury Lane,
My master he was good to me, my mistress was the same.
When along came a sailor ashore on liberty,
And oh, to my woe, he took liberties with me.

Chorus
Singing bell-bottom trousers, coat of Navy blue,
Let him climb the rigging like his daddy used to do.

It was at a ball I met him, he asked me for a dance.
I knew he was a sailor by the way he wore his pants.
When the ball was over he asked to see me home,
Then asked if he could stay the night as he was all alone.

He asked me for a candle to light his way to bed.
He asked me for a handkerchief to tie around his head.
Me a foolish maiden, not thinking it no harm,
I jumped into the bed with him to keep the sailor warm.

He really was no Samson but that night he went to town.
He laid me on the bed there till my blue eyes turned to brown.
Early next morning the sailor he awoke,
And the crafty bastard handed me a crabby ten bob note.

Saying, 'Take this my darling for the damage I have done,
'For if it be a daughter or if it be a son.
'If it be a daughter, jounce her on your knee,
'But if it be a son, send the bastard off to sea.'

Now come all you young maidens and listen to my plea,
Don't ever let a matelot get an inch above your knee.
I trusted one once and he put out to sea,
And left me with a daughter to jounce upon my knee.

Jounce: To bump, bounce, jolt (fifteenth century, of unknown origin)
(OED).

94 *Abraham the Sailor*

'Who's that knocking at the door?'
Said the fair young lady.
'It's only a son come home from sea,'
Said Abraham the Sailor.
'If you'll wait one minute I'll let you in,'
Said the fair young lady.
'Oh where am I going to sleep the night?'
Said Abraham the Sailor.

'You can sleep in bed with me,'
Said the fair young lady.
'There is no room for two in the bed,'
Said Abraham the Sailor.
'You can sleep on top of me,'
Said the fair young lady.
'Oh what is that thing that looks so black?'
Said Abraham the Sailor.
'That's my pin-cushion,'
Said the fair young lady.
'I've got a pin and I'll stick him right in,'
Said Abraham the Sailor.
'If you do I'll call the police,'
Said the fair young lady.
'Bugger the police and fuck the Force,'
Said Abraham the Sailor.

A more polite commercial version of this song emerged in the 1930s
under the title 'Barnacle Bill the Sailor'.

95 *The Whale Island Anthem*
(Fragment)
('Cruising Round Yarmouth')

I've fought with the Russians,
I've fought with the Boers,
But never no more with an old Chatham hag. ('whore', or 'those old
Chatham whores'?)

Chorus
Fal lor I addie, fal lor I addie,
Fal lor I addie I addie I hey.

My magazine's empty.
My powder's all spent,
I can't fire the gun 'cos there's shit in the vent.

Chorus
Fal lor I addie, fal lor I addie,
Fal lor I addie I addie I hey.

96 *The Hat Me Old Man Wore*
(Tune: 'The Hat My Father Wore')

Good evening to you one and all,
Good luck to you I say.
I've just come here to see you now
Before I go away,
And I've brought with me a relic
Of past happy days of yore,
When I strolled through Dublin City
In the hat me old man wore.

Chorus
Sure, it's old and it's shabby,
But I love it just the same,
For McGinty brought it over
When from Ireland first he came.
It brings to me the memory
Of bright happy days of yore,
When I strolled through Dublin City
In the hat me old man wore.

When first I joined the Navy
'Twas the first hat that I wore,
But the old hat was not uniform
On a British man-o'-war,
So I lashed it up in me hammock
As I sailed the brine seas o'er,
And that accounts for the present state
Of the hat me old man wore.

You can have your nice cheese-cutters
And your broad-brimmed bonnets fair
Your fancy man-o'-war hats
And your ribbons and your stars.
You can search the China Station
From Shanghai to Singapore,
But you'll never find another
Like the hat me old man wore.

Now messmates take this good old hat
And treat it with respect.

> Don't sling it in the scranbag,
> Or boot it about the deck,
> Or the ghost of Guinness'll haunt ye
> As you sail the brine seas o'er,
> And you'll curse the day you trampled on
> The hat me old man wore.

The contributor's comments are of interest:

> In case it's of any use I have scribbled out an old song which I
> learned from a Chatham dockyard matey in 1919. He was ex-Navy
> and a Battle of Jutland survivor. If I remember rightly he said he
> learnt it from a man whose father or grandfather wrote it. Not
> sure. There was a pub, 'The Dutchman', at Old Brompton not a
> great way from the Dockyard at Chatham where quite a few Navy
> and ex-Navy types used to gather for a sing-song. This Jutland
> survivor used to play a flute and sang quite a bit too.

97 *We'll Have Another Dance Until the Boat Comes In*
(Tune: 'The Sailor's Hornpipe')

> Tiddly om pom pom did you ever see the Queen?
> Have you ever seen a sailor sloshing a marine?
> If you go to Gib-er-altar take a flying jump to Malta
> And we'll have another dance until the boat comes in.

Another form of the first two lines was:

> Hi there Jack, have you ever seen the Queen?
> Have you ever seen a Blue-Jack kissing a marine?

The contributor mentions that his father often used this as a
'dandling' song in the mid-1940s. At other times he would amuse
his offspring by dancing a sailor's hornpipe while singing it, and
something very similar, 'We'll Have Another Drink Before the Boat
Shoves Off', was used for the same purpose, when no instrumental
music was available, by deepwater sailing men in the later years of
the China tea clippers according to William Doerflinger in *Shantymen
and Shantyboys* (Macmillan, New York, 1951, p. 167).

98 *Flash Cows of the City*
('The Sailor Cut Down in His Prime')

One night, very late, through the Dockyard I wandered,
When I met me a messmate all staggering and drunk.
He asked for assistance to help him to bed,
And early next morning he was found lying dead.

Chorus
We played the pipes lowly, we beat the drums slowly,
We played the 'Dead March' as we bore him along,
And then at his graveside three volleys fired o'er him
In memory of a matelot cut down in his prime.

At the top of this street you will see two girls standing.
One to the other was heard to remark:
'Here comes the young sailor whose money we've wasted,
'Whose life we have tasted and wasted away.'

Now there on his tombstone these few words were written:
'All you young sailors take heed of these words
'And don't go a-courting flash cows of the city.
'Flash cows of the city brought me to my grave.'

Also known to modern sailors as 'The Matelot Poxed Up in His Prime'. The graceful final couplet of the second verse seems to be a rare example of a twentieth century improvement on older texts, and is all the more remarkable because this stanza was obtained from a teenage Royal Marine Reservist at Plymouth around 1959-60. He had learned it from his sergeant back home on Merseyside. Another contributor recalls:

In the last war (1939-45) I have seen the Fleet Canteen at Scapa
Flow hushed and still whilst this song was sung, accompanied by a
Royal Marine bandsman playing – of all things – a violin and, of
course, passing around his hat for beer money.

99 *This Old Hat of Mine*
('All For Me Grog')
(Tune: Various, including 'Maggie May')

This old hat of mine,
The inside is quite new
The outside it has seen some stormy weather,
So I cast this hat aside
For I mean to travel wide,
Far across the sea I mean to wander.

Subsequent verses substitute other articles of clothing, 'jumper', 'vest', 'pants,' 'shoes' and so on, in place of 'hat', with each item being discarded at the appropriate moment. It was customary for the performer to stand on a table and when no more clothing remained to have his nether regions drenched with his shipmates' beer.

Lastly we come to a very durable favourite, though one whose honest sentimentality (it was described by one informant as a 'last-half-hour-in-the-wet-canteen type') gradually became less and less fashionable as the 1900s progressed, until now it is rare to hear it performed with appropriate sincerity. Its style indicates an origin outside the Royal Navy, probably from the pen of a professional song-writer ashore, but I include it here because, after several generations of transmission through performance, it has become reasonably 'folklorised', and must now be regarded as having undergone a process of oral re-creation sufficient to earn it at least tentative recognition as a Royal Naval folk song. To demonstrate this satisfactorily, however, would entail reproducing a succession of available textual variants for comparison. Instead I give merely the set of words which seem to me the most complete, and possibly as old a form as we can expect to find now.

The late Bob Roberts informed me that an early reference to the song crops up in a Midshipman's log book kept by an ancestor of his mother whilst serving in HMS *Narcissus* (steam and sail) in 1860. The story could refer to the Indian Mutiny, although so-called 'Naval Brigades' involved in military operations ashore were not uncommon elsewhere around this time. Later versions sometimes have the hero meeting his death in a more orthodox way, in a sea battle.

100 *You'll be Happy Little Sweetheart in the Spring*
(Tune: See Appendix D)

On a lovely summer's evening, when all the world was still,
Two lovers wandered hand in hand beside an old wood mill.
He was leaving on the morrow for a land so far away,
And as she nestled close to him she heard her lover say:

Chorus
You'll be happy little sweetheart in the spring.
Those wedding bells for you will surely ring.
And when England's shores are sighted
Our two hearts will be united.
You'll be happy little sweetheart in the spring.

On the quay there stands a matelot in his uniform so neat.
He's waiting for the picket-boat to take him to the fleet.
Then the sirens start a-blowing, to the mast the pennants fly.
As the cables rattled down below she heard her lover cry:

Chorus
You'll be happy little sweetheart in the spring.
Those wedding bells for you will surely ring.
And when England's shores are sighted
Our two hearts will be united.
You'll be happy little sweetheart in the spring.

Now the scene is changed again, alas, 'tis on a battlefield.
Our boys in blue are fighting hard the glorious flag to shield.
When a stray shot hits our hero and he's numbered with the slain.
As his shipmates gathered round the lad they sang this sad refrain:

Chorus
You'll be lonely little sweetheart in the spring.
Those wedding bells for you will never ring.
For your sailor lad is lying
Among the dead and dying.
You'll be lonely little sweetheart in the spring.

In a cottage sits a maiden who is weary, worn and sad.
The tears come rolling down her cheeks, a letter she has had.
And as she reads the letter the pain is hard to bear,
And long before the morning breaks she's left all worldly care.

Chorus
So they laid her in the churchyard in the spring.
Those wedding bells for her did never ring.
Not a word of him was spoken
For they knew her heart had broken
As they laid her in the churchyard in the spring.

Appendix B

SHARED REPERTOIRE

The point made in the Introduction concerning songs shared by all three fighting Services, and in some cases other units of society too, is best demonstrated by the following examples. Some, though deliberately adapted by the sailor to give them an apparent 'pure Navy' flavour, were also to be found in their Army and RAF versions. Others were sufficiently general or non-Service in content for them to be heard in much the same form whether in Navy canteens, Sergeant's Messes, RAF Nissen huts, or anywhere else.

101 An AA Gunner Lay Dying
(Tune: 'Wrap Me Up in My Tarpaulin Jacket')

An AA gunner lay dying
At the end of a midsummer's day.
His comrades were gathered around him
To carry his fragments away.

The mounting was piled on his wishbone,
The breech-block was wrapped round his head,
A shell stuck out of his elbow,
It was plain that he'd shortly be dead.

He spat out a toggle and rammer
And stirred in the oil where he lay.
Then to his poor mournful comrades
These brave parting words did he say:

'Take the rollers out of my stomach,
'Take the breech-block out of my neck,
'Remove from my kidneys the handwheel.
'There's lots of good parts in this wreck.'

'Take the chase out of my gullet,
'Take the interceptor out of my brain,
'Extract from my liver the striker,
'And assemble the pom-pom again.'

'I'll be riding a cloud in the morning,
'And aircraft no more shall I fear,
'And high on a cloud over Scapa
'I'll shed all my good friends a tear.'

'So don't mourn too much over my body.
'Damn old Hitler and all of his lies.
'Here's a health to the dead already.
'Let's hope he's the next one who dies.'

102 *My Girl from Battersea*
(Tune: 'My Home in Tennessee')

My girl from Battersea
Means all the world to me.
Tattooed from head to knee,
She's a lovely sight to see.
Under her jaw
Is the Royal Flying Corps,
And on her back is the Union Jack,
Now who could ask for more?
And up and down her spine
Are the Coldstream guards in line,
And on her shapely hips
Is a fleet of battleships.
Tattooed on each kidney
Is a bird's-eye view of Sydney.
Around the corner
The Johnny Horner,
My girl from Battersea.

136

103 10th MTB Flotilla Song
(Tune: 'The Church's One Foundation')

We are Fred Karno's Navy,
No bloody good are we.
We cannot fight, we cannot fuck,
We cannot go to sea,
But when we get to Malta
You'll hear the C-in-C:
'Mein Gott, mein gott, what a bloody fine lot
'Are the boys from the MTB.'

Said the contributor:

The 10th MTB Flotilla in 1941 had a song which might interest
you. The boats were, basically, World War One coastal motor
boats, and had already proved themselves dangerously unreliable
mechanically in UK waters, including Dunkirk. In January 1941
the flotilla was freighted to the Middle East, round the Cape, but
Malta still represented the Mediterranean Station to sailors, and all
were convinced we should end up there. In fact, virtually the
whole flotilla was blown up in Suda Bay shortly after arrival in
Port Said. Two, which broke down on passage, were subsequently
sunk in Tobruk, and only one boat ever reached Malta where,
needless to say, it was promptly sunk with all hands. The last time
I heard our flotilla song it was being howled out in the streets of
Alexandria from the back of a three ton truck in which the
survivors from Crete were being taken to the transit camp before
being split up.

104 We are but Little Sailors Weak
(Tune: 'We Are But Little Children Weak')

We are but little sailors weak.
Our pay is fourteen bob a week.
The more we do, the more we may,
It makes no difference to our pay.

Our hours per day are twenty-four.
We thank the Lord there are no more,
For if there were I'm sure that we
Would work another two or three.

In the late 1930s an able seaman received less than a farm labourer, a junior postman or a government typist under the age of twenty-one. Petty officers earned less than engineering labourers and about as much as government typists aged twenty-three. Even taking account of total emoluments in cash and kind, an able seaman got no more than about £2 14s a week, while a skilled tradesman ashore was likely to draw more than £4 6s.

(Anthony Carew, *The Lower Deck of the Royal Navy 1900–39*, Manchester University Press, 1981)

105 *The Brothers St John*
(Tune: See Appendix D)

We
Are
Two Irish Maltese,
We come from the Island of Gozo.
The first time we met, it was down in Vallett.,
We are two Irish Maltese.

Chorus
We're the twins, tinga linga ling,
We're the twins, tinga linga ling,
We're the Brothers St John and you know where we're from,
When we're out
There's no doubt
We're so much alike in our figure and height.
As we stroll along on the prom
The brass band plays tiddly-om-pom.
They say as we pass, 'There go two blades of grass,'
Me and my brother St John.

In the summertime, you know,
To the seaside we go,

Where the air is so fresh and so bracing.
We sing and we shout when there's no one about,
Me and my brother St John.

Chorus

The above is the least lewd assemblage of elements from various versions that I have been able to manage, but I assure aficionados of the song that, composite though it may be, the text is authentic throughout, and there has been no bowdlerisation.

106 *My Brother Sylvest*
(Tune: See Appendix D)

Have you heard about the big strong man
Who lived in a caravan?
Have you heard about the Johnson–Jeffrey fight,
When the big buck nigger fought the white?
You can bring all the heavyweights you've got,
But I've got a lad to lick the lot.
In the morning he rings the bell in the belfry
And tonight he fights Jack Dempsey.

Chorus
That's my brother Sylvest,
Got a row of forty medals on his chest,
Fought forty niggers in the West,
He takes no rest.

CHANT
   Bigga da man! Stronga da push!
   Hell fire! Son of a gun!
   Eyes in the boat! Keep stroke!
   In rake! Out bake!
   What's yours? Mine's a pint!
   Cook o' the mess! Don't make us shit!
   Stand back! Don't push!
   Plenty o' room for you and me.

He's got an arm
Like a hip,
And a punch that would sink a battleship.
It takes all the Army, Navy, Air Force and Marines
To put the wind up Sylvest.

Now he thought he'd take a trip to Italy,
And he thought he'd make the trip by sea.
So he dived into the harbour at New York
And he swam like a fish made of cork.
Saw the big ship *Lusitania* in distress,
So he swallowed all the water in the sea,
Took the big ship *Lusitania* on his chest,
And he walked all the way to Italy.

Chorus
Now he thought he'd take a trip to old Japan,
So they turned out the old town band.
He played all the instruments they'd got,
And he buggered up the whole damn lot.
The old church bells they were ringing,
And the old church choir they were singing.
They all turned out to say goodbye
To my brother Sylvest.

Chorus

The words have been given without the customary interpolations by the audience in the many convenient gaps caused by the rhythm of the tune, and only a selection of the wide variety of improvisations in the 'chant' have been presented. Some experts could go on for a minute or more.

There is little resemblance left between these traditional words and the original lyrics of Jesse Lasky and Sam Stern, though I have received a small scrap of the earlier work from a 1914–18 veteran, and Fred Fisher's music to which they were written has been abandoned altogether in favour of a fresh, traditional tune.

In recent years 'My Brother Sylvest' has been rediscovered by singers of the British folk song revival, their belated enthusiasm producing more than a little wry amusement among people reared in naval ports and garrison towns who had absorbed the song, along with the air they breathed, from their earliest days without ever realising that it was such a dark secret to so many others.

107 *Sod 'em All*
(Tune: 'Bless 'em All')

Sod 'em all, sod 'em all,
The Skipper, the Jimmy and all.
Sod all the Yeomen and CPO Tels.,
Sod the Chief Sloshies and their bleeding smells
For we're saying goodbye to them all
As back to their hammocks they crawl.
You'll get no promotion this side of the ocean
So cheer up my lads, sod 'em all.

Sod 'em all, sod 'em all,
The Jaunty, the Crusher and all.
Sod all the Shipwrights and CPO Cooks,
Sod all the Paybobs and their bleeding books
For we're saying goodbye to them all
As back to their hammocks they crawl.
You'll get no promotion this side of the ocean
So cheer up my lads, sod 'em all.

Sod 'em all, sod 'em all,
The Admiral, the Flag-Jack and all.
Sod all the OAs and EAs as well,
Sod the Chief Stoker and send him to hell
For we're saying goodbye to them all
As back to their hammocks they crawl.
You'll get no promotion this side of the ocean
So cheer up my lads, sod 'em all.

This may or may not be a vulgar parody of an innocuous popular wartime song. It is not generally realised that 'Bless 'Em All', like 'Barnacle Bill the Sailor' (see No. 94) was a toned-down version of a coarser original. C. H. Ward-Jackson, in *The Airman's Song Book* (William Blackwood, 1967) draws attention to the fact that although the forerunner of the commercial 'Bless 'Em All' had been the unofficial trooping song of the RAF since 1918 it actually originated in the Royal Naval Air Service in 1916, written by Fred Godfrey. It is possible that the version given above is a direct linear descendant of that original, but it could equally well be a straightforward re-working of the Second World War popular song. In either case the quite substantial verse section has been dispensed with and the chorus section developed into stanzas.

Appendix C

FRAGMENTS

While not denying the likelihood that many of the 'songs' presented in the main body of the collection are incomplete or perhaps mere fragments of more substantial creations, it can at least be claimed that each is capable of standing on its own as a finished product even if the remainder of the work is never recovered. Other scraps have come my way, however, which are so curtailed or moth-eaten as to be unpresentable even on this basis. Yet these are frequently the most fascinating items of all because, though they may make sense to some degree, the overall context is tantalisingly absent.

It occurred to me, therefore, to put some of these lyrical potsherds on display in the hope that here and there the memory of some reader may assist in the task of restoring the whole artefact before yet another precious piece of the Royal Navy's song heritage is washed down the scuppers of time. My titles are purely arbitrary, of course.

108 When the Flagship 'Victoria' went Down

He was a loving companion,
He was a faithful friend.
In sunshine and stormy weather
On Jack you could always depend.
He sailed on the seas from his childhood,
On his face there was never a frown.
I lost the best friend that ever I had
When the flagship *Victoria* went down.

Now Jack and I were shipmates
From the first time that we went to sea.
Now both at work and pleasure
Now Jack he was good company.
He was a loving companion,
And he was a faithful friend,
But I lost the best pal, yes, that ever I had
When the flagship *Victoria* went down.

Now picture his old aged mother,
She is sitting by the cottage door,
And she's knitting socks for her loved one
She expected soon ashore.
When they told her the news of the disaster
She cried out, 'It cannot be true,
'For I've just received a letter saying
'He'll be home in a week or two.'
Then they told her his grave was the ocean,
She cried out and fell to the ground.
'I've lost the best son, and the only one,
'If the flagship *Victoria's* gone down.'

During fleet exercises off the Lebanese coast on 22 June 1893 HMS *Victoria*, flagship of the Mediterranean fleet, was accidentally rammed by HMS *Camperdown* and sank with great loss of life, including that of Admiral Tryon himself. Many of the crew came from the Portsmouth area, and this song was reputedly printed and sung in that locality to raise money for the bereaved families. It was said to have been banned officially, due to one verse being openly critical of the Admiral. It has no connection with the 32-verse contemporary 'poem for recital' entitled 'The Loss of HMS *Victoria*' by W. A. Eaton.

109 *The Grey North Sea*

And oh, we peppered them hot, sir,
And yelled aloud with glee,
Till the enemy staggered back to port
In the grey North Sea.

This is said to be about the Battle of Jutland.

110 *Send out the 'Chryssy'*

Send out the *Chryssy*,
The *Moy, Ouse* and *Issy*,
But for God's sake don't send me!

Obviously the conclusion of a parody of the First World War song
'Send Out the Army and the Navy'. The subject (of the parody) is
early morning gunnery practice in the Mediterranean, and I
understand many of the ships in the Mediterranean Fleet were
mentioned. The ones whose names we have *Chrysanthemum, Moy, Ouse*
and *St Issy*, were, I think, target towing vessels.

111 *The West Atlantic Squadron*

Here we come, sword and drum,
Here we come, full of rum,
Looking for something to wallop the bum
Of the West Atlantic Squadron.

Described by the contributor as 'the tag of a very ribald nonsense of
which I wish I knew the rest.'

112 *The Sailors they are Going Away*

The sailors they are going away.
They won't be back for many a day.
They've put all the girls in the family way
To fight for England's glory.

113 *Shore Sailor*

Shore sailor, shore sailor, pull for the shore.
Pull like a son-of-a-bitch but don't break the oar.
Safe in the lifeboat, clinging to sin no more.
Leave the dreary sinking wreck and pull for the shore.

Based on the chorus of 'The Lifeboat', Sankey No. 99.

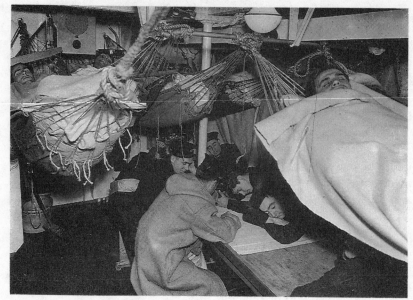

'Beautiful dreamer, lash up and stow'

114 Lash Up and Stow
(Tune: 'Beautiful Dreamer')

Beautiful dreamer, lash up and stow,
'Cooks to the galley' went ages ago.

115 Angels of Queen Street
(To a hymn tune)

Angels of Queen Street
All dressed in white.

Appendix D
SOME TUNES

The modern sailor is not unique in being more gifted as a weaver of lyrics than as a creator of melodies. Consequently most of the foregoing verses, it will be seen, are wedded to already existing tunes. But, as indicated in the Preface, there are a few exceptions. In the following pages will be found transcriptions of tunes which, as far as I can ascertain, belong only to the words given. They are, in short, folk melodies, probably of a later vintage than most that have been collected in this century. In transcribing them I have, for the reader's sake, tried to avoid complicated keys.

1. *That's What it's Like in the Navy*

7. *She's a Tiddley Ship*

10. *On the Booms*

13. *Sammy Ring the Bell*

38. I Hopped up to the Gangway

40. Gosport Nancy

42. Sailors' Wives

48. 'Baa!' Go the Goats

60. *The Noble Eighth of December*

92. *A Matelot and a Pongo*

100. You'll be Happy Little Sweetheart in the Spring

105. The Brothers St John

106. My Brother Sylvest

SOURCES

CT Indicates that a version of the song was assimilated naturally by the author at some time or other in the course of his life, and was not acquired through a formal act of collecting.

NR Indicates either that the name of the contributor was not recorded at the time the song was collected, or that the correspondent–contributor did not supply his or her name.

No. of song

1   Ernest Davies, Bingley, W. Yorks, 1984.
2   A.S.E. Tawney, Gosport, Hants (author's father).
3   M.J. Golightly, Bath, from an article in the *Hampshire Telegraph*, 1959, reproduced by courtesy of *The News*, Portsmouth.
    T.W. Townsend, Wanstead, London.
    J.A.G. Lamb, Salisbury, Wilts.
4   T.W. Townsend, Wanstead, London.
5   Stores PO Cock, HMS *Murray*, 1958.
    M.J. Golightly, Bath (as No. 3).
    C.E.S. Collier, Wimbledon.
    Cdr D.J. Bradby, RN, Soberton Heath, Hants.
    G.L. Green, Ealing, London.
6   John Powell, Maiden Newton, Dorset.
7   PO Steward Thomas, HMS *Murray*, 1958
    W. Thurgar, Cooksville, Ontario, Canada.
    Cdr D.J. Bradby, RN, Soberton Heath, Hants.
    LSA (V) Bryan Bush, HMS *Nubian*,
    G.H. Glasly, Liphook, Hants.
8   LSA (V) Bryan Bush, HMS *Nubian*.

9   NR.

10   Josh Starkey, Saccone & Speed's warehouse, Plymouth Barbican, 1959.

11   H.S. Johnson, Stubbington, Hants.

12   A.S.H. Tawney, Ashton-under-Lyne (author's brother).

13   NR, HMS *Collingwood*, Fareham, Hants., New Year's Eve, 1958.

14 ⎫
15 ⎬ John Lucas-Garner (via Philip Barker, Birmingham, 1969).
16 ⎭

17   NR, Hill Park Hotel, Plymouth, 1968.

18   Reg Rich, Keynsham, Bristol, 1985.

19   Printed (anon.) in 'HMS *Cheviot*, The Last Commission, May 1958 – October 1959', but the late Drew Lees assured me he had heard it sung on other ships as well.

20   LMA Geoff Kirk, 1967.

21   Geoff Kirk (ex-LMA), Glasgow, 1985.

22   C.E.S. Collier, Wimbledon.

23   A.S.E. Tawney, Gosport.
     Peter Cotterill, Hastings, Sussex.

24   NR.

25   CT, Barry L. Jones, Warrington.

26   Barry L. Jones, Warrington.

27   Original text from John Bush, Walsall, 1966. Other variants from Ernest Davies, Bingley; 'Sharkey' Ward; Stores PO Cock, HMS *Murray*, and many others.

28   W. Taylor, St. Albans. He first heard it at Devonport Barracks in 1923.

29   L.A. Densham, Gosport, 1960.

30 ⎫
31 ⎬ Eric Drummond, Leeds, 1985.

32   CT.

33   Geoff Kirk, Glasgow, 1985.

34   Andrew Lees (via Geoff Kirk, Glasgow, 1985).

35   J. Redford, Middlewich, Cheshire.

36   LSA(V) Bryan Bush, HMS *Nubian*.

37   NR, Plymouth, 1960.

38   J.A.G. Lamb, Salisbury, Wilts.

39   LSA (V) Bryan Bush, HMS *Nubian*.

40   NR, at a folk song evening, Cecil Sharp House, London, 1960.

41   NR, at a Hampstead restaurant, 1959.

42   Clare Clayton, Brighton, 1970. Learned from her father, Valentine KilBride (sic), an RN signalman in 1914–18 war. Published in 1971 by EFDS Publications (*Folk Songs of Today* No. 5)

43 Ned Hammond, Holt, Norfolk, 1965 (via Peter Kennedy). Cdr D.J. Bradby, RN, Soberton Heath, Hants.

44 A.S.E. Tawney, Gosport.
NR, Cherry Tree Inn, Plymouth, 1959.

45 CT; Mike Sadler, Southampton, 1961.
NR, Forester's Arms, Plympton St Maurice, Devon, 1960.
Cdr D.J. Bradby, RN, Soberton Heath, Hants.
Ivor Burston, Wiveliscombe, Somerset, 1985.

46 Barry L. Jones, Warrington.

47 Jan Ridler, RN Armament Depot, Ernesettle, Plymouth, 1962.

48 Charlie Baird, Birmingham 1986. Learned from his father, Lt Cdr Tom Baird RN. Also published, with non-traditional, composed verses added, in *The Navy Song Book* compiled by Inglis Gundry.

49 NR, HMS *Orion*, Reserve Fleet, Devonport, 1959.
Royal Fleet Auxiliary seaman named 'Cisco', Cherry Tree Inn, Plymouth, 1959.

50 REA Peter Gogerly, HMS *Murray*, January, 1958.

51 Cook(S) 'Tug' Wilson, HM Submarine Auriga, July 1970.

52 CT; John Powell, Maiden Newton, Dorset.

53 J.A.G. Lamb, Salisbury, Wilts.

54 J. Redford, Middlewich, Cheshire.

55 NR; LSA(V) Bryan Bush, HMS *Nubian*.

56 NR, RNA Club, Devonport, 1962.
LSA(V) Bryan Bush, HMS *Nubian*.

57 CT; ERA Jack Smith, HMS *Orion*, Reserve Fleet, Devonport, 1959.
Barry L. Jones, Warrington.

58 C.E.S. Collier, Wimbledon.

59 NR 1960 Original text of 'Revenge' from Mr A.M. Palmer, Swansea, 1980.

60 Rock Berntsen (Falkland Islander), Southampton, 1985. He can be heard singing it on *Kelpers After All* (Forest Tracks FT3017).

61 L.B. Horton (via Capt. P.L. Gunn, DSM, RN, Sudbury, Suffolk).

62 } J.A.G. Lamb, Salisbury, Wilts.
63 }

64 Bill Foster, Camberwell, London (via Shep Woolley, 1983).

65 Kenneth H. Bond (via Brian Patten, BBC Bristol 1963).
CPO Roberts, HMS *Cambridge*, Wembury, Plymouth (via John Morrish).
A.J. Spilstead, Portsmouth, 1966.
Roy Morris, Keighley, Yorks.
J.T. Atter.

66 D.J. Edworthy, Totnes, Devon (via *Western Morning News*).

67 W.F. Wiley, Vancouver Naval Veterans' Association, Canada, 1967.

F.R. Anthony, Sutton Coldfield, W. Midlands, 1985.

68 *Royal Navy Song Book*, compiled during Second World War by Inglis
Gundry who says the song originated in one of the 'O' class
destroyers.

69 NR, Leicester, 1962.
W.F. Wiley, Vancouver Naval Veterans' Association, Canada, 1967.
Mick Bugden, Swadlincote (HMS *Savage* Association).
Capt. J. Cunningham DSC, RN, 1985. Capt. Cunningham confirms
that verses 1, 3, 4, 6 and 7 of the text I give were in the original set
composed by himself and his colleagues. In fact he was the 'crazy
Number One' in verse 7, which he composed in collaboration with Lt
Larry Taylor, the 'wretched Pilot'.

70 Eric Drummond, Leeds, 1985.

71 Bob Moses, Liverpool, via Eric Drummond, Leeds, 1985.

72 NR, 'Lion and Column', Plymouth, 1960.
LSA(V) Bryan Bush, HMS *Nubian*.

73 H.J. Lockey, Stockton on Tees. Published in *Folk Roundabout*,
Summer 1983.

74 M.J. Golightly, Bath (as No. 3).

75 Lewis Johns, Plymouth, 1963.
Colin Taylor, Yeovil, 1969.
NR, St Albans Folk Club, 1968.
Lt-Cdr W.A. Murray RNVR (via Peter Cotterill, Hastings).
Cdr D.J. Bradby RN, Soberton Heath, Hants.
Ruth Cooper, Portsmouth.

76 Ruth Cooper, Portsmouth.
F.W. May, 'Queen's Head', Albaston, Cornwall.

77 Ruth Cooper, Portsmouth.

78
79 } Gordon P. Smith, Birmingham, 1969.
80

81 J.A.G. Lamb, Salisbury, Wilts.

82 POM(E) Terry Moriarty, Elladia Club, St Budeaux, Plymouth, 1962.
C.E.S Collier, Wimbledon.
Lt 'Paddy' Ryan RNVR (via Albert Craven, Leeds, 1982).
Mick Jones, Newton-le-Willows, 1985.

83 Jan Ridler, RN Armament Depot, Ernesettle, Plymouth, 1962.

84 From *One of Our Submarines* by Edward Young (Rupert Hart-Davis,
1952). For evidence that this was in oral circulation among
submarine crews, see *Submarines at War 1939–1945* by Alastair Mars
(William Kimber, 1971), Chapter XI.

85 Albert Craven, Leeds, 1982.
Mick Jones, Newton-le-Willows, 1985.

86
87 } Mick Jones, Newton-le-Willows, 1985.

88   CPO Telegraphist 'Jan' Cryer, HMS *Dolphin*, Gosport, 1958. Angus
     McHutchon, Southport, 1974.

89   Cook (S) 'Tug' Wilson, HM Submarine *Auriga*, 1970.
     Ken Penney, Jolly Porter Folk Club, Exeter, 1972, 'Collated by
     H. Tait, Clyde Submarine Base, Faslane, Scotland, 1969'.

90   Ruth Cooper, Portsmouth.

91   NR.

92   NR, Newcastle-on-Tyne, 1959.
     ME Sid Porter, HMS *Tiger* and Padstow, Grecian Club, Plymouth,
     1967.

93   LSA(V) Bryan Bush, HMS *Nubian*.
     Ron Sallis, Wolverhampton, RNA and others NR.

94   ERA Jack Smith, HMS *Orion*, Reserve Fleet, Devonport, 1959,
     collected by him in the 'Avondale' pub, St Levans Gate, Devonport.

95   T.W. Townsend, Wanstead, London.
     J.A.G. Lamb, Salisbury, Wilts.

96   F.C. Fairbrass, Helston, Cornwall.
     Also fragment from Tim Walsh, Devonport, 1959.

97   J.B.P. Penney, Bill Radford, both via Ken Penney, Tiverton, Devon,
     1972.

98   Lt W.W. Griffiths, RN, Havant, Hants.

99   CT; R.B. Buckle, Norwich.
     F.R. Anthony, Sutton Coldfield, W. Midlands, 1985.

100 AB Fred Corrigan, HMS *Orion*, Reserve Fleet, Devonport, 1959.
     P.E. Robinson, Deal, Kent.
     Bob Roberts, Ryde, IOW.
     Bertha Brown, Worksop, 1985.
     Roy Palmer, Birmingham, 1985.

101 Lt F.H. Spendelow (SCC) RNR, Newport, Mon.

102 Eric Drummond, Leeds, 1985.

103 Capt. C.C. Anderson RN, Director, Royal Naval Careers Service,
     MOD, 1966.

104 J.A.G. Lamb, Salisbury, Wilts.

105 A.S.E and A.S.H. Tawney.
     'Petty Officer', HMS *Forth*, Singapore.
     R.W. Thrower.
     Tom Mills, Westbury-on-Severn, Gloucs.

106 Phyllis Pearce (author's aunt), Gosport.
     E.V. Hutchinson.
     G.H. Glasly, Liphook, Hants.
     Anne Fisher, Gosport.

Capt. P.L. Gunn DSM, RN, Sudbury, Suffolk.
Barry Jones, Warrington, and others NR.
107 W. Thurgar, Cooksville, Ontario, Canada.
108 F. Norrish, Crediton, Devon, 1970.
Johnny Doughty, Rye, Sussex (via Roy Palmer, 1985).
109 Roy Palmer, Birmingham, 1984.
110 L.A. Densham, Gosport, 1960.
111 Cdr R.D.P. Hutchinson RN, Farnham, Surrey.
112 ⎫
113 ⎭ Eric Drummond, Leeds, 1985.
114 CT.
115 Peter Terson, Romsey, Hants.

GLOSSARY

Many of the slang and technical terms used in the songs are explained incidentally in the accompanying text, but for ease of reference it has been thought advisable to set out here as complete a list as is reasonably possible of those words and expressions that are likely to need explaining to the non-naval reader. However, those words which can be found in any good standard dictionary, and these include most terms from the days of sail, have generally not been included here. The numbers in brackets refer to the songs in which a word or expression occurs.

AC-IC (68) Possibly an officer with responsibility for aircraft identification, or perhaps Admiral Commanding Iceland or Icelandic Convoys.
ALT (77) Probably Approach Landing Trials, but possibly Air Launched Torpedo.
Ash-rake (74) See 'Devil'.
ASV (77) Air to Surface-Vessel, an early radar fitted under the Swordfish.
Bandy (43) Bandmaster.
Barra (75) Fairey Barracuda. Reputedly a very unreliable aircraft.
Battery-boards (82) Fitted boards covering the main batteries in the old conventional type of submarine. They could be removed in sections to gain access to any particular part of the battery, but when in position they actually formed part of the internal corticene-covered deck upon which the crew not only walked but, as in the song, often slept.
Black-list (38) A list of naval ratings who were either facing a minor charge or were already undergoing punishment such as extra work or drill, stoppage of leave, etc. (see 'Nines').
Blacks put up galore (77) To 'put up a black' was an aviator's expression, derived from the RAF, meaning to blunder, to make a mistake, or commit a misdemeanour, i.e. to do something that merited a 'black mark'.
Bloke, the (38) The Commander, a warship's senior executive officer. To be

brought 'before the Bloke' was to be placed in the Commander's Report as a defaulter.

Blow(s) (82) The apparatus by which air is forced into a submarine's ballast tanks to expel water. Used in conjunction with 'vents' (q.v.) they control a submarine's buoyancy.

Bootneck (13) A Royal Marine. Also known as 'Leatherneck' (see No. 43), especially in the United States Navy as applied to their own Marines. In earlier times Royal Marines' tunics were held together at the throat by a leather fastening which, according to the impish imagination of their Royal Navy comrades, had been fashioned out of the tongues of sailors' boots.

Bradbury (38) A pound note. Named after Baron Bradbury (1872–1950) who, as John Bradbury, was Secretary to the Treasury from 1913 to 1919. At the outbreak of war in 1914 he realised that the imminent scarcity of gold would seriously affect Britain's financial machine unless something was done. His answer was a very swift issue of paper money of a conveniently small denomination to replace gold. A facsimile of his signature appeared on the notes, which for many years after were known as 'Bradburys'.

Buffer (32) Chief Boatswain's Mate, though he was often known as the 'Chief Buffer', with the Petty Officers under him referred to as 'Buffers'. The most popular explanation seems to be that as he was the Commander's right-hand man and gave effect to his orders concerning work done about the upper deck he was acting as a kind of buffer between that officer and the seamen. But the term has a long history in the Royal Navy, and in *The Slang Dictionary* (1864) it is suggested that, as one of the Boatswain's Mate's former duties was to administer the 'cat', the word may derive from 'buff', meaning bare skin. However, the verb 'to buff', from the Norman-French 'buffe' meaning a blow (as in 'blind man's buff'), is an obsolete form of 'to buffet' or strike a blow, and in that sense, earlier generations of Chief Boatswain's Mates would surely have been well worthy of the appellation 'buffer'.

Burgoo (28) Porridge. Of Middle Eastern origin, the word has been in use in both the Army and the Navy for over 200 years.

Casing (81) That part of a submarine, excluding the bridge, which is visible when the vessel is on the surface. It is non-watertight and serves mainly as a cat-walk to facilitate external passage from one part of the submarine to the other.

Cell flat (38) A 'flat' is an open area below decks lined on either side with a number of adjacent cabins or compartments. In this case the compartments are the cells where prisoners are kept.

Chief, Chiefy (14, 15, 17, 27, 73) A Chief Petty Officer. (43) The Engineer Commander or the senior Engineer Officer. As a rule 'Chief' is heard more often than 'Chiefy' in the Wardroom.

Chippy (19) Ship's Carpenter, a Shipwright.

Chokker (69) The Navy's equivalent to the civilian term 'fed up'.

Clacker (45) Pastry.

Coaling rig (4) Old worn-out clothing which, instead of being discarded, was kept especially for coaling ship.

Commander (F) (76) Commander Flying.

Commission (7) When a warship is newly-built or has completed a major dockyard refit she takes on her full complement of officers and men and is then 'commissioned' at a special ceremony. From that moment until the day her complement is 'paid off' in preparation for another major refit she is said to be 'in commission'. When a sailor says he 'commissioned HMS "So-and-So"' he means he was a member of her very first crew. He will also use the term 'foreign commission' to describe a spell of duty overseas, whether ashore or afloat. As used in No. 75, however, the meaning is the one normally understood ashore, that of a 'percentage' or 'rake-off'.

CPO (107) Chief Petty Officer. A point of interest is that where a non-naval person will say 'CPO' as written, i.e. as a set of three initials, Navy people, or those who are much in their company, always read it as 'Chief PO'. The first word is never abbreviated to an initial in speech.

Crabby (20, 89, 93) Dirty.

Crabs (38) Navy Issue boots.

Crusher (56, 107) Regulating Petty Officer. A member of the 'Ship's Police', the Regulating Branch. From the 'beetle- or cockroach-crushers' which he wears on his feet throughout the day.

Devil, Ash-rake and Slice (74) Implements for dislodging and removing clinker and ashes from the furnaces in coal-burning ships.

Dhoby (20, 22) Wash one's clothes, bedding, hammock, etc. From the Hindustani 'dhobi'. 'Dhobying' is personal laundry.

Dip (38) 'Dip him one Good Conduct badge' means to deprive him of it. For an explanation of the significance of Good Conduct badges see 'Stripey'.

Director (49) Part of a ship's automatic gunnery control system.

Dirk (43) Where other officers carried a sword with full dress uniform a midshipman would carry a dirk.

Di-so (20, 48, 49) A Maltese 'water-taxi', similar to a gondola. 'Di-so' is a phonetic representation of the British pronunciation. The correct spelling is 'dghaisa'.

Doing cells (42) Serving a period in detention, usually either on board ship or in barracks.

Doz (55) Short for 'dozen', meaning the conclusion of a twelve-year engagement in the Royal Navy.

Draft-chit (27) A notification on paper that a sailor is being posted ('drafted') to another ship or establishment. 'Draft' in the Royal Navy does not mean 'compulsory call-up' as it does in the USA.

Drink (75) The sea.

Dual (75) Dual training with an instructor, as opposed to flying solo.

Dustman (16, 74) Stoker, from the days of coal-burning ships when he would be covered in coal-dust.

EA (107) Electrical Artificer.

Fifteen-inch (49) Fifteen-inch gun. The heavy armament of a battleship.

Fire and bilge (19) Pumps used for removing excess water from the bilges. Also used in fire-fighting.

Five (3) The conclusion of a five-year engagement in the Royal Navy.

Flag-Jack (107) Flag Lieutenant. On the staff of an Admiral, where he attends to the signal staff and the Admiral's social commitments.

Flatfoot (74) Seaman. Probably derived from the days when so many of them went barefoot about the upper deck for so long that they acquired large flat feet as a result.

F.O.2 (75) Attempts to identify this aircraft have been unsuccessful. Some type of reconnaissance plane seems to be implied. However, it has been suggested by Lt.Cdr. Norman Dubery RNVSR, of Leeds, that 'F.O.2' may have been a misreading of 'F.O.11', even though '2' is necessary for the sake of rhyme. The F.O.11 was a Fleet Observation Aircraft. They were, in fact, Fairey Battles brought 'out of retirement'. Their armament was removed and cameras were fitted. It was customary for any aircraft that was 'improvised' in this way to be given the Mark number '11'.

FOGT (78) Flag Officer Ground Training.

'Formid'. (75) The aircraft-carrier HMS *Formidable*.

Forty-two (47) Forty-two days detention (in the 'mansion up the hill').

Gargle (40) General slang for a drink, but used by sailors to refer to rum.

Gash (28) Leftovers where food is involved, but also meaning anything going spare, or refuse.

GI (90) Petty Officer Gunnery Instructor, the Navy equivalent to the Army's Drill Sergeant.

Grey Funnel Line The sailor's nickname for Royal Navy ships, after the manner of merchant shipping lines and passenger lines.

Guzz (55) Devonport, Devon. The origin is as obscure as is 'Pompey' for Portsmouth.

HO (66) 'Hostilities Only'. A rating who joined the Royal Navy for the duration of the war and no longer.

Hydroplanes (82) Movable fins situated on either side of the bows (foreplanes) and stern (afterplanes) of a submarine. When the craft is submerged and under way any deviation from the horizontal transmitted to these fins will affect the angle, and therefore the depth, of the submarine. At 'diving stations' and during an attack the Coxswain mans the afterplanes and controls the depth, while the Second Coxswain mans the foreplanes and controls the angle of the submarine, although the two work in co-ordination and not independently.

166

Jagger (45) More correctly 'Jacker' ('Cousin Jack'), a Cornishman.
Jago's, Jago's Mansion (27, 28) Devonport Barracks. Early this century a Warrant Officer by the name of Jago introduced the General Messing system into the Royal Navy at Devonport. It was considered a great improvement on the earlier system (see 'Scran Chum'). The food became known as 'Jago's' and the mess-hall, and subsequently the barracks as a whole, earned the nick-name 'Jago's Mansion(s)'.
Janner (55) A native of Devon ('Cousin Jan'), but more particularly in Naval circles anyone from the Plymouth area.
Jaunty (24, 27, 47, 54, 107) Master-at-Arms, the senior rating in the Regulating Branch (the 'ship's police'), with overall responsibility for lower-deck discipline. Derived from the French 'gendarme'.
Jenny Wren (56, 57) A member of the WRNS, the Women's Royal Naval Service.
Jimmy, Jimmy the One (1,5,6,7,20,43,54,86,87,107) The lower-deck name for the First Lieutenant.
Jossman (39) Master-at-Arms, possibly because he is 'God' on the lower deck.
Killick (32) A Leading Hand. That is, a Leading Seaman, Leading Stocker, Leading Telegraphist, etc. Strictly speaking a 'killick' is another name for an anchor, which is the badge worn by the Leading Hand on his left sleeve.
KR's and AI's (90) King's Regulations and Admiralty Instructions. The Statutes of the Royal Navy.
Lash up (38, 39) This term basically means 'give', either in the sense of 'donate' or 'stand treat' (38) or 'impose' (39).
Lash up and stow (17, 114) One of the first things a sailor did after getting out of his hammock in the morning was to 'lash it' by tucking in the bedding and passing a long length of rope known as a 'hammock lashing' round and round the hammock at uniform intervals by means of marline-hitches. The regulation number of turns was seven. The hammock was then 'stowed' in a special rack known as a 'hammock netting'.
Leatherneck (43) See 'Bootneck'.
Liberty (73) Short for 'liberty boat', the craft which takes ashore those ratings eligible for shore leave ('libertymen'). They usually run at specified times which are prominently displayed (the 'boat routine' which the Doctor's wife carries in No. 43). Even where an actual boat is not needed, such as in shore establishments or a ship alongside a dock wall, ratings may still be required to leave in orderly groups at certain laid-down times, and these are still called 'liberty-boats'. If this routine is relaxed and ratings allowed to make their way ashore individually in their own time it is termed 'open gangway'.
Loose-lead line (42) It has not been possible to identify what is meant here, but the term may refer to a boat lead and line as distinct from a deep-sea lead.

Make and mend (87) An afternoon off, a half-holiday, though not necessarily including shore leave. In former times, before ready-made clothes were issued, this was the best opportunity for the sailor to make and mend his clothes.

Middle watch (14) From midnight to 0400 hrs (4.00 a.m.). The least popular watch with most people because it is virtually impossible to get a sound sleep either before or after the watch. This is officially acknowledged inasmuch as it is customary for those with the middle watch to be entitled to a 'make and mend' (q.v.) the following day.

Nines (39) This has no connection with the 'Number Nines' (laxative tablets) mentioned in song No. 31. The severity of naval punishment was graded by numbers, with the lower numerals denoting the harsher retribution, Number One being the death sentence. Number Nine punishment consisted of a combination of stoppage of leave, pre-Reveille calls, extra work during leisure periods and mustering at stipulated times calculated to cause the maximum inconvenience.

Number One (15, 69, 80) Number One boiler (15). The Wardroom term for the First Lieutenant (69, 80).

OA (107) Ordnance Artificer.

OD (49, 66) Ordinary Seaman. Presumably to have used the initials OS would have led to confusion with Officer's Steward.

Oggie, Oggy (45) Cornish pasty. Short for 'Tiddy-Oggie'. Paradoxically the term is now in more common use among sailors than among the populace of Devon and Cornwall. The origin of the term has never been satisfactorily established.

Oggin (9) The sea.

Oppo (8, 33, 34) Close friend. Short for 'Opposite number'. Originally, back in the days of the two-watch system, the term referred to the person in the opposite watch who, by virtue of holding the same qualifications and being of the same status as himself, was the person a rating approached if he wanted someone to 'stand in' for him when his duty watch came round, to enable him to go ashore. At some later date this favour would be reciprocated, and what sociologists call a 'gift relationship' would build up. Ironically, due to being in opposite watches, the opportunities for these original 'oppos' to go on a run ashore together were few and far between, which is not the case with the 'oppos' of today.

Patches (43) The white patches worn by a midshipman on his upper lapels.

Paybob (107) Lower-deck term for the Paymaster.

Pig (15) This derisory lower-deck nickname for a naval officer was in use generations before it was appropriated by delinquents and activists as a synonym for a policeman.

Pilot (43, 69) The Wardroom nickname for the Navigating Officer.

Plates (16, 19, 42) The various platforms made up of iron deck-plates to be found in ship's engine-rooms and boiler-rooms (16). A panel of steel which, when rivetted to other similar sections, forms the ship's side (19) or a boiler (42).

PO (16, 66) Petty Officer.

Pongo (92) Soldier. As to the origin of the name, a number of suggestions have been put forward, to which I would like to add one more. In his *Dictionary of Phrase and Fable* the Rev. E. Cobham Brewer, after stating that the original 'Pongo' was a legendary amphibious monster of Sicily, slain by the three sons of St George, goes on to say that it was also 'a loose name for African anthropoid apes'. The derivation seems to be from the Congolese name 'mpongi'. For a very long time now there has been established on the Rock of Gibraltar a colony of large, tailless monkeys from North Africa known as 'Barbary Apes'. In my own time I have often heard sailors refer to the soldiers permanently stationed at Gibraltar as 'rock-apes'. Is it not possible that a much earlier generation of matelots used Brewer's term 'pongos'? It would only have been a matter of time before the name lost its purely Gibraltarian associations and became applied to soldiers in general.

Pride of Keyham (27) Steamed pudding. Keyham is a district of Devonport. The Royal Naval barracks is situated there.

PST (19) When a rating passed the Navy Swimming Test these initials were entered in his pay-book.

PTI (43) Physical Training Instructor.

Pusher (36) A young woman. From 'pram pusher'.

Pusser('s) (38, 43, 55, 56, 74, 90) A corruption of 'Purser', the ship's Supply Officer (in the same way that 'cuss' derives from 'curse'). Hence any item of Navy property could be prefixed with the adjective 'pusser's': a knife is a 'pusser's dirk', boots are 'pusser's crabs', and so on. Without the possessive ending ('pusser') it describes a person or a course of action adhering strictly to Navy regulations.

Queries (36) The Pay Office was open at strictly limited times for ratings to query the pay they had received.

Rabbit (56) Any item or commodity rightfully the property of the Admiralty (or, later, the Ministry of Defence) which is smuggled ashore. The act of doing so is called 'rabbitting'. For a plausible theory concerning the origin of the term see Wilfred Granville's *Dictionary of Sailor's Slang* (Andre Deutsch, 1962). A secondary meaning has developed in more modern times whereby the name 'rabbit' is applied to any present brought home from abroad.

RNB (27) Royal Naval Barracks.

Round-down (75, 80) The after-end of an aircraft-carrier's flight-deck, which curved downward at this point. An aircraft coming in to land approached the flight-deck from this end.

Scale (38) An automatic minimum punishment for overstaying one's leave.

For every three hours or part thereof that a rating was 'adrift' he lost one day's pay and one day's leave at least. If the offender had a bad record for being late off leave, or if there were other aggravating circumstances, punishment could be increased, 'in addition to the Scale'.

Scran bag (38, 96) Sailors are trained to stow everything away in the lockers and other receptacles provided, not just for the sake of neatness but, in the event of a compartment flooding, to prevent any floating articles, especially clothing, from blocking an outlet or fouling up machinery. If, during an inspection ('rounds'), any items were found 'sculling' about, they were confiscated and placed in the 'scran bag', sometimes an actual bag but usually a locker, until redeemed on 'payment' of a quantity of ship's soap or a fine. The bag was originally used to collect waste food, hence the name. The sense of the last line in No. 38 seems to be garbled.

Scran chum (38) When a mess was responsible for its own catering ('canteen messing') it was the responsibility of two ratings each day to decide on the day's menus. As the pairing was a fairly permanent one they were known as 'scan chums' or 'scran oppos'.

Seafire (75) A version of the Supermarine Spitfire modified for operating with the Fleet Air Arm.

Shit, In (7), (89) and (95) the meaning is simply 'dirt'. To be 'in the shit' (39) is to be in trouble. Where the word is used elsewhere the orthodox dictionary meaning is intended, though not always literally.

Shit-hot (92) Drunk. The term also means 'excellent', and in its bibulous sense probably refers to the feeling of euphoria associated with intoxication.

Shooting (69) Gunnery practice.

Slice (74) see 'Devil'.

Slops (38) Although originally meaning a sailor's working clothes, 'slop' signifying 'very cheap', 'ready-made', the term now means any item of kit sold from the ship's clothing store or 'slop-chest'. Unfortunately, due to the confused nature of what is probably an incomplete and imperfectly remembered text, the sense of 'pail of slops' in No. 38 is not easy to interpret with confidence.

Sloshy (107) More correctly 'slushy', a cook. 'Slush' was the grease left after boiling the salt pork eaten by seamen in the days of sail. One half of this slush was the cook's perquisite and was kept in the 'slush tub'. An examination of the text of No. 107 will show that the poor Chief Cook has been dished out with a double helping of invective!

Snotty (43) Midshipman. Generally explained with reference to the habit these young officers had of wiping their noses on the cuffs of their uniform jackets, to prevent which the Admiralty decreed that buttons were to be sewn on that part of the sleeve. However, *The Slang Dictionary* of 1864 points out that 'snot' was 'a term of reproach applied to persons by the vulgar when vexed or annoyed', which suggests an alternative derivation.

Soldier (43) The Wardroom nickname for a Royal Marine officer.

Spirit room (92) The compartment on board ship which is used as a rum store.

Splinter-box (19) A method of dealing with a moderate inflow of water in a bulkhead or ship's side. A steel T-piece is passed outside the hole and a steel box bolted to it on the inboard side. The box can then, if necessary, be shored up for extra strength.

Sprog (92) Child. Also used as a nickname for new recruits. Which usage came first is debatable.

Stanchion (27) Someone who has managed, by accident or design, to avoid sea-time and remain in barracks for a very lengthy period. In full, 'barrack stanchion', implying that he has become indispensable to the continuing existence of that establishment.

Standing part (38) Although a sailor would sometimes use this expression when referring to his wife, in contrast to extra-marital girl friends, in a more general sense it meant anything permanent or unchanging (it is actually the non-moving rope in a purchase). Here perhaps the reference is to the rubber band, or whatever, that has been holding the pound notes together.

Starry-gazy pie (45) Cornish pilchard pie with the fishes' heads protruding through the 'clacker' (q.v.).

Station card (33) Upon joining a ship or shore establishment every member of the lower deck was issued with a small card containing such details as his name, ship's paybook number and the watch to which he belonged. It was in effect a 'membership card' of that particular ship or establishment, but worked in reverse. It was not needed to get in, but to get out. A 'libertyman' had to deposit the card at the ship's gangway or establishment Regulating Office before proceeding ashore, and collect it again on his return. In this way it was always known which ratings were still ashore. It was also needed for 'pay parades' and was such a precious item that sailors referred to it as their 'breathing licence'. Should a rating commit a misdemeanour the first thing a superior would do, even before arraigning him on a charge, was to demand the surrender of his station card, effectively stopping his shore leave until his case had been settled one way or the other. Despite the song's levity, to use another person's station card amounted to impersonation and could lead to serious consequences for both parties.

Stripey (43, 49) Below the rank of Chief Petty Officer a rating would wear, on the upper part of his left sleeve, the badge of his rank, or 'rate', namely cross-anchors for a petty officer, a single anchor (see 'Killick') for a leading hand, or no badge for those below this rank. In addition he would wear, if entitled, up to three good conduct stripes, showing length of 'good conduct' service, or 'undetected crime' as the sailors usually put it. Formerly one was awarded after three years, a second after eight years and a third after

171

thirteen years, but this was later changed to four years for each stripe. They did not denote rank as in the other Services and could be awarded or taken away (see 'Dip') without affecting a person's status, although a certain small increment of pay was involved. They were popularly known as 'badges', and a rating would be referred to as a 'no-badge', 'one-badge', 'two-badge' or 'three-badge' PO, 'Killick' or 'Sod-all'. An ordinary rating with the maximum three good conduct chevrons (a 'three-badge Sod-all') may never have risen in rank or may have been reduced after some offence. Either way he was known to his messmates as 'Stripey'. An old messdeck rhyme, obviously more popular with younger sailors than with veterans, ran:

> Two badges gold
> Too bloody old
> Three badges red
> Bloody nigh dead.

Stroppy (66) Argumentative, unruly, obstreperous. The latter word is often mispronounced 'obstroperous' or 'obstropalous' and 'stroppy' is probably a contraction of this.

Subby (75) Sub-lieutenant.

'Swain (20, 82) Short for Coxswain. Submarines carry both a Coxswain and a Second Coxswain (informally addressed as 'Scratch' or 'Scratcher'), hence the plural in No. 82 (see 'Hydroplanes').

Tel. (107) Telegraphist. A CPO Tel. was a Chief Petty Officer Telegraphist.

Three-badge (50, 90) See 'Stripey'.

Tickler (20, 55) Naval duty-free tobacco or, as in No. 55, cigarettes made therefrom. The tobacco was supplied in tins manufactured by a firm named Tickler's, who also supplied the Navy with jam and marmalade.

Tiddley (7) Smart, spick-and-span. A sailor's 'tiddley suit' is his number one shore-going uniform.

Tiffy (15, 18, 82) Artificer.

Tombola (73) The Naval name for the lottery game known ashore as 'Bingo', 'Housey-housey' or 'Lotto'.

Torp (43) Torpedo Officer. Before the creation of a specialist Electrical Branch in the Royal Navy he was also in charge of the ship's electrics.

Tot (1, 11, 40, 92) The one eighth of a pint measure of rum per day to which all ratings over the age of twenty were at one time freely entitled if they so chose.

UJC (54) The Union Jack Club, near Waterloo station, London.

Under-cart (77) An aircraft's under-carriage.

Vent(s) (82, 86) Apertures in the top of a submarine's ballast tanks which can be opened to allow air to escape when flooding and closed to allow air pressure to discharge water through the flood-holes when 'blowing' the tanks (see 'Blows').

(95) 'Vent' here means the touch-hole of the gun.

Walkashore A series of pontoons and gangways connecting a ship with the shore. If circumstances, e.g. shallow water, prevent a ship from actually securing alongside a jetty or other recognised landing place, a walkashore does away with the necessity for liberty boats.

Watch below (2) The off-duty watch.

Water rats (38) River police, but here the term may mean the shore patrol.

Wavy Navy (76) The Royal Naval Volunteer Reserve, whose officer's gold braid was in the form of a wave instead of the straight rings of the regular Navy.

'Western' (27) The *Western Morning News*, a Devon and Cornwall daily newspaper.

Winger (49) Originally this meant a young novice sailor taken 'under the wing' of a veteran, usually a 'Stripey' or Petty Officer. It might or might not imply a homosexual bond. Often it was a perfectly innocent father/son type of relationship, with the junior partner referring to the senior as his 'sea-daddy'. Later the term came to mean simply any close friend (often addressed as 'wings'), or someone's assistant.

Wings (75) Commander (Flying) of an aircraft carrier or naval air station, who was responsible for the flying activities of squadrons under his command and controlled all flight-deck or runway operations.

WT (77) Wireless telegraphy, morse code transmission equipment.

Yeoman (107) Yeoman of Signals, who held a Petty Officer's rate. Above him was the Chief Yeoman of Signals, holding a Chief Petty Officer's rate.

INDEX

174

175

STERNPIECE

Collections are illusory things. Though they are often the outcome of years of very occasional gleanings of a sparsely distributed item, yet, gathered together in one place, whether it be a book, a museum or a gallery, they convey the impression of abundance. Thus, because of the diligent work of several individuals such as Cecil Sharp and Sabine Baring-Gould, certain counties of Britain are popularly believed to have been the home of more folk songs than other counties; a book-full of rustic songs gives the armchair reader a false picture of a singing peasantry warbling from dawn to dusk. And it is much the same with the old collections of sea songs. Because men like Ashton and Whall applied themselves to the task of gathering the material into a volume it does not necessarily follow, as some think, that the Victorian needed only to tap a passing sailor on the collar and he would straightway launch into half a dozen stirring traditional sea ballads. Now that my own collection is published no doubt the pendulum of opinion will overswing again, so that where before all agreed the matelot's muse had perished by the time of the *Dreadnought* so it will now be the common belief that every second bluejacket strolling out of the dockyard gate heads for the nearest tavern for an evening of traditional matelot's ditties. Nothing could be further from the truth. Song-hunting will always be a difficult and demanding hobby, but I hope I have demonstrated that, in the case of the Royal Navy at least, it will never be a futile one.

Cyril Tawney